AUTISM
TREATMENT
GUIDE

3rd Edition

Eliza

FUTURE HORIZONS INC

Future Horizons, Inc.
Arlington, Texas

IMPORTANT:

This book is for informational purposes only; the author does not endorse any treatments described. Before beginning a new treatment for yourself or your child, consult a physician. The author disclaims any liability arising directly or indirectly from the use of the book.

The author is grateful for permission to reprint the following copyrighted material:

Excerpt from the *Diagnostic and Statistical Manual of Mental Disorders, Fourth Edition*, copyright © 1994. Used by permission of the American Psychiatric Association.

Excerpt from "Autism: Basic Information." Used by permission of the New Jersey Center for Outreach Services.

"Definition of Autism" used by permission of the Autism Society of America.

Library of Congress Catalog Card Number 93-91648

ISBN-1-885477-99-6

Designed by Eugene Print, Inc.

Jacket Photo: Karen Esperanza

Published by: Future Horizons, Inc.
                721 W Abram St
                Arlington, TX 76013
                (800) 489-0727

Printed in the United States of America

TABLE OF CONTENTS

Foreword v

Acknowledgments vi

Author's Note vii

Autism Defined 1

Diagnosis 3

Tests 21

Education 27

Nutritional Supplements 49

Biomedical Interventions 59

Dietary Interventions 71

Anti-Yeast Therapy 83

Sensory/Physical Therapies 89

Intensive Interventions 107

Music Interventions 117

Relaxation Techniques 123

ATEC List 131

Appendix: Organizations 133

Index 149

Also by Elizabeth King Gerlach

"Just this Side of Normal:
Glimpses Into Life with Autism"

Winner, Autism Society of America
"Outstanding Literary Achievement of the Year, 2000"

For Robert and Dylan
and other four-leaf clovers in the field.

FOREWORD

When Elizabeth Gerlach first told me about this project, I was thrilled that someone, finally, was going to organize an incredible amount of information into a well-balanced, clear and concise book. She was able to accomplish this task, and as a result, the *Autism Treatment Guide* has become one of the best-selling books in the field of autism.

I also like the overall attitude of the book: "What's the bottom line?" Many parents want to learn about ways to help their children, and the format of this book allows them to find relevant information in an efficient manner along with references and contact numbers. I know many "network" parents throughout the country, and many of them keep a copy of this book on their desk to use as a handy reference guide.

Autism is a heterogeneous disorder, ranging from low to high cognitive functioning and from mild to severe behavior problems. Consequently, there is no recipe, no "one way" to help these children. I feel it is important for parents and professionals to be aware of the available treatments and to learn as much as possible before beginning a treatment program.

I truly believe that the more stimulation you give to these individuals, the better their prognosis. I hope parents and professionals will use this book as a guide on the road to helping individuals with autism.

— Stephen M. Edelson, PhD.
Director, Center for the Study of Autism

ACKNOWLEDGMENTS

Without the help and support of many wonderful people, this book would have remained only an idea. I would like to thank Jane Novick, not only for her editing expertise, but also for opening her heart and home to my whole family and for being a most wonderful friend.

I also wish to thank Dr. Stephen Edelson, Director of the Center for the Study of Autism, for reviewing this work, and encouraging and supporting me in this endeavor, not once, but twice!

Thanks to The Autism Society of America and the Autism Research Institute for helping parents like me understand autism, and for providing us with the information and support we need to help our children with autism.

Also my gratitude to Jane and Ken Austin, Leslie King, Clayton King, and F.E. McNeil for technical assistance, art-work, and support, and to Joan Cookson for assistance with the printing. Thanks to all the many professionals (Svea Gold, Rob O'Neill, Dr. Skye Weintraub, Kathleen Hogan, Kelly Oatman, and Gita Wertz, who read the material for accuracy of content; Valda Fields for the vote of confidence. Thanks to Patricia Marucci for her willingness to lend an ear or a hug, and to Janine Fisher, for her inspiring energy and effort. I thank Jean B. Yates for being like a sister to me and for her true grit. Thanks to Eric Bottjer, an excellent writer, who believes in my work as I do in his. For my compassionate co-workers at Rainbow Valley— chocolate kisses with almonds. Thank you, Wayne Gilpin, for being a mentor to me all these years.

Many thanks to Rand, for his support of my writing and his devotion to our family. Finally, special thanks to my children, who are my greatest teachers.

AUTHOR'S NOTE

As a parent of a child diagnosed with autism, I have talked with parents, gone to workshops, picked the library clean, and I still keep my eyes and ears open for ways to help my son. But what I've needed all along is a book that has information on treatments in one accessible place. I needed it to know what was available to help my son when he was first diagnosed. I wasted a lot of "early intervention" time by being unaware of treatment options. While certain treatments may be more effective if our children are younger, our quest for helping them is a life-long endeavor. To do this, we must be aware of the possibilities. I've found the adage, "knowledge is power," a motto to live by as I raise my child with special needs.

I am an optimist and a realist. I know there are no "miracle cures" for autism. Yet, I am not afraid to dream of the day when there might be. I can still hold on to that dream even if it is with the nail on my little finger.

What I don't like is people telling me what I should or shouldn't try as a means to help my child. Therefore, this book offers only straightforward information and *does not endorse any treatment*. If you are a parent, I respect you as the expert on your child, and I trust you to choose the treatments that are right for your child. If you are a professional, I urge you to respect a parent's judgment, even if you disagree, and to be as supportive as you can. Please don't blame us parents for trying, for hoping.

Regarding treatments for autism, what works wonders for one individual may have absolutely no effect on another. I wish I could say, "This really helped my son, maybe you should try it," but that would be setting a lot of you up for disappointment. What makes a successful treatment? To me, a successful treatment improves the quality of my son's life or my family's life, often in small but significant ways. Say we try a particular treatment, and my son sleeps through the night for the first time in his life, but he still wakes up autistic. I say that treatment is a success; if we are well rested everyone benefits. But what if I try a method that takes time and patience to follow through, but ultimately I see no results? I give myself credit for trying to help and I move on without regrets.

I think it is important for people to realize that treatments can and should be combined. For instance, experts warn that medications should not be given as a substitute for a consistent behavior management program. Likewise, sensory integration therapy could be incorporated into a child's school day if it helps him or her handle stressful situations. While I think it is important for purposes of research to know what treatments make a noticeable difference, once this has been established why not combine them as you try to improve the quality of your life or the life of your child.

I realize that information is constantly changing. As soon as this book is printed someone will have changed a phone number or a zip code. Yet I hope it can be of help to you. I don't claim to have included every treatment that could help someone with autism. I know that having kids with autism swim with dolphins shows promise, but the closest most of us can get to that one is renting *Flipper* at the video store. Now there's an idea . . .

Elizabeth King Gerlach
Eugene, Oregon

Autism Defined

For years, children with autism were thought to have emotional problems or to suffer from schizophrenia. We now know that this is not true. Autism is a physical disorder characterized by specific symptoms that vary in kind and severity with each individual. **The following definition of autism is reprinted here from the Autism Society of America.**

What is Autism?

Autism is a complex developmental disability that typically appears during the first three years of life. The result of a neurological disorder that affects the functioning of the brain, autism and its associated behaviors have been estimated to occur in as many as 1 in 500 individuals. Autism is four times more prevalent in boys than girls and knows no racial, ethnic, or social boundaries. Family income, life-style, and educational levels do not affect the chance of autism's occurrence.

Autism interferes with the normal development of the brain in the areas of social interaction and communication skills. Children and adults with autism typically have difficulties in verbal and non-verbal communication, social interactions, and leisure or play activities. The disorder makes it hard for them to communicate with others and relate to the outside world. They may exhibit repeated body movements (hand flapping, rocking), unusual responses to people or attachments to objects, and they may resist changes in routines.

Over one half million people in the US today have some form of autism. Its prevalence rate now places it as the third most common developmental disability—more common than Down syndrome. Yet most of the public, including many professionals in the medical, educational, and vocational fields, are still unaware of how autism affects people and how to effectively work with individuals with autism.

Diagnosis

Autism is a confusing disorder because it presents itself in unique ways in each affected individual. Some children with autism may show severe cognitive impairment, whereas others may show incredible skills in math, memory, or art, but are severely lacking in social skills. Some individuals cannot speak, whereas others are verbal, although their speech may lack meaning to those around them. Many individuals with autism insist on sameness in their environment, exhibit repetitive behaviors such as rocking, engage in routinized, unimaginative play, and seem to be aloof or unaware of their environment and the people in it.

Dr. Leo Kanner was one of the first professionals in the field of psychiatry to identify children who exhibited autistic characteristics as a separate group from those labeled schizophrenic. Yet it has taken decades for professionals to recognize and understand the nature of autism. Dr. Bernard Rimland's book, *Infantile Autism:*

The Syndrome and Its Implications for a Neural Theory of Behavior, published in 1964, broke ground in the area of autism. It debunked the assumption that autism was a result of "bad" parenting, and it helped to establish autism as a neurobiological disorder.

Although the degrees of severity vary greatly from individual to individual, one common thread among those with autism is the impairment of communication skills in a social context. Lack of eye contact, rigid or concrete thinking, difficulty in processing information, sensory problems, anxiety, and echolalic speech are just a few of the factors that may interfere with an individual's ability to create reciprocal social interactions.

Autism is behaviorally defined. There are no medical tests that can be administered to establish a diagnosis of autism, although tests can rule out or identify other underlying problems. In order to determine a diagnosis of autism, professionals depend on observation of the behavioral characteristics of each individual. Basically, the more autistic behaviors a person exhibits, the more likely it is that they will be diagnosed as having autism.

Obtaining a correct diagnosis can be a major hurdle. Most experts in the field of autism would agree that an evaluation conducted by an interdisciplinary team is the ideal choice when autism is suspected. Such an evaluation team consists of professionals from a variety of specialty areas working together to determine a diagnosis. The team may include, but is not limited to, a psychologist, a pediatrician with knowledge of autism, an educational diagnostician, a speech/language pathologist, an audiologist, and perhaps a social worker. Parents play a critical role in the process of diagnosis by providing information on the child's developmental history and behaviors. Because autism is a behaviorally defined disorder, it stands to reason that the more professionals who observe the behaviors at various times and in various settings, the better the chance of making an accurate diagnosis of autism; it is certainly better than having one specialist evaluate alone.

To determine a child's disorder, professionals must also determine what disorders are not present. The comparison of the behaviors of the child being diagnosed with behaviors typically seen in other disorders is known as "differential diagnosis." Mental retardation and/or language disorder are two major disorders that must be investigated. The child is also tested for medical and genetic problems, such as Phenylketonuria (PKU) and Fragile-X Syndrome, which are sometimes seen in conjunction with autism.

When evaluating a child with developmental problems, doctors and psychologists often use the American Psychiatric Association's Fourth Edition of the *Diagnostic and Statistical Manual of Mental Disorders* (DSM-IV, 1994), which outlines criteria for identifying most disorders, both mental and emotional. Autism falls under the subclass, "Pervasive Developmental Disorders." For "Autistic Disorder," the DSM-IV lists twelve diagnostic criteria falling into three major categories: impairment in social interaction, impairments in communication, and a restricted repertoire of activities and interests. The diagnosis of autism is made if the child displays at least six of the 12 symptoms and a minimum number in each category. Also, the onset of these symptoms must have occurred during infancy or early childhood.

Some individuals with autistic-like behaviors may not meet all the criteria for a diagnosis of "Autistic Disorder"; in this case, they are sometimes given the diagnosis, "Pervasive Developmental Disorder Not Otherwise

Specified" (PDDNOS). Many researchers feel that the term "pervasive developmental disorder" is inaccurate and unfair. Individuals with autistic-like symptoms who are diagnosed with PDDNOS may not be given the legal rights of those with autism. Many professionals feel that autism is not a "pervasive" disorder, but one in which "specific" social/cognitive skills are impaired. Meanwhile, professionals will continue to use the criteria set forth in the DSM-IV, which is continually revised to reflect changes in criteria for various disorders.

Researchers are working to devise new ways of testing for autism in very young children. These tests may prove to be an extremely valuable tool because early intervention may make a significant difference in the treatment of individuals with autism. Such a test, developed by researchers Simon Baron-Cohen, Jane Allen, and Christopher Gillberg, is the "Checklist for Autism in Toddlers" (CHAT). Questions on this test regard social interactions, imaginative play, communication skills (verbal and nonverbal cues), and imitation. This 14-question test is given to parents and physicians familiar with the child. In the first controlled study, researchers tentatively identified four out of 91 children (all 18-months old) who were all later positively identified with autism at 30 months of age. [See Allen, pp. 839-43.]

The Autism Research Institute distributes a diagnostic checklist, known as Form E-2, first published in 1964, which was designed primarily as a screening instrument to help researchers identify children with autism for participation in research studies. Also, Form E-2 is designed to help in the process of diagnosing children who have been labeled autistic, autistic-like, schizophrenic, or PDDNOS. Only five to ten percent of children labeled autistic fit the description of early infantile autism as defined by Leo Kanner in 1943. Parents or professionals complete the questionnaire, giving answers based on behaviors the child exhibited between the ages of three and five. The Institute scores the child on both behavior and speech patterns and combines these for a total score. The child is scored on a scale ranging from -45 to +45. Any score above +20 indicates a probable case of early infantile autism. Children who score from -15 to +19 are typically regarded as autistic by professionals. Children whose scores are -16 or lower are usually described as "autistic-like" (or labeled with some similar term). Scoring is done at no charge, and results are returned to the parents or professionals who submitted the form.

Sometimes, parents of a child with a disability must rely on an evaluation conducted by their school district. Educators often use the Childhood Autism Rating Scale (CARS) to evaluate children with autism. [See Schopler, et al.] If parents have doubts or questions concerning the outcome of this evaluation, parents may seek further evaluations from outside the school system. If the results differ, the school district is legally responsible for payment of the private evaluation, unless it can prove at a due process hearing that the district's evaluation was appropriate. The school district must consider the results of a private evaluation when making decisions concerning the child.

There are other syndromes, such as Tourette Syndrome, Rett Syndrome, and Asperger's Syndrome, in which characteristics of autism are often present. Professionals are moving toward identifying subgroups of autism. Meanwhile, researchers continue to search for genetic links, environmental factors, abnormalities in brain structure, and/or neurobiological factors that may contribute to autism and related disorders.

The American Psychiatric Association's *Diagnostic and Statistical Manual of Mental Disorders* (Fourth Edition) lists these criteria for **299.00 Autistic Disorder:**

A. A total of six (or more) items from (1), (2), and (3), with at least two from (1), and one each from (2) and (3):

(1) qualitative impairment in social interaction, as manifested by at least two of the following:

(a) marked impairment in the use of multiple nonverbal behaviors such as eye-to-eye gaze, facial expression, body postures, and gestures to regulate social interaction

(b) failure to develop peer relationships appropriate to developmental level

(c) a lack of spontaneous seeking to share enjoyment, interests, or achievements with other people (e.g., by a lack of showing, bringing, or pointing out objects of interest)

(d) lack of social or emotional reciprocity

(2) qualitative impairments in communication as manifested by at least one of the following:

(a) delay in, or total lack of, the development of spoken language (not accompanied by an attempt to compensate through alternative modes of communication such as gesture or mime)

(b) in individuals with adequate speech, marked impairment in the ability to initiate or sustain a conversation with others

(c) stereotyped and repetitive use of language or idiosyncratic language

(d) lack of varied, spontaneous make-believe play or social imitative play appropriate to developmental level

(3) restricted repetitive and stereotyped patterns of behavior, interests, and activities, as manifested by at least one of the following:

(a) encompassing preoccupation with one or more stereotyped and restricted patterns of interest that is abnormal either in intensity or focus

(b) apparently inflexible adherence to specific, nonfunctional routines or rituals

(c) stereotyped and repetitive motor mannerisms (e.g., hand or finger flapping or twisting, or complex whole-body movements)

(d) persistent preoccupation with parts of objects

B. Delays or abnormal functioning in at least one of the following areas, with onset prior to age 3 years: (1) social interaction, (2) language as used in social communication, or (3) symbolic or imaginative play.

C. The disturbance is not better accounted for by Rett Disorder or Childhood Disintegrative Disorder. [Reprinted with permission from the American Psychiatric Association.]

The DSM-IV also presents a description of **299.80 Pervasive Developmental Disorder Not Otherwise Specified (Including Atypical Autism):**

This category should be used when there is a severe and pervasive impairment in the development of reciprocal social interaction or verbal and nonverbal communication skills, or when stereotyped behavior, interests, and activities are present, but the criteria are not met for a specific Pervasive Developmental Disorder, Schizophrenia, Schizotypal Personality Disorder, or Avoidant Personality Disorder. For example, this category includes "atypical autism"—presentations that do not meet the criteria for Autistic Disorder because of late age at onset, atypical symptomatology, or subthreshold symptomatology, or all of these. [Reprinted with permission from the American Psychiatric Association.]

Other disorders having characteristics in common with autism:

• **Asperger's Syndrome**...Symptoms include coordination deficits, depression, repetitive speech, monotonic voice, dislike of change, like of routine and rituals, inability to relate "normally" to people. Most individuals have IQ scores in the normal range.

• **Fragile-X Syndrome**...A genetic condition in which there is a constriction on the long arm of the X chromosome. Most individuals with Fragile-X Syndrome have mild to moderate retardation. Often present are repetitive motor behaviors, oversensitivity to sound, dysfunction in verbal and nonverbal communication, and cognitive processing problems.

• **Landau-Kleffner Syndrome**...Children develop normally for the first three to seven years, and then there is a rapid loss of language skills. Often these children are misdiagnosed as deaf. EEG readings are used to determine whether or not a person has Landau-Kleffner Syndrome. Autistic-like behaviors include attention deficits, insensitivity to pain, echolalic speech, and impaired motor skills.

• **Moebius Syndrome**...Causes many nervous system problems (including paralysis of the facial muscles, which leads to vision and speech difficulties) as well as behavioral problems like those associated with autism.

• **Rett Syndrome**...Usually seen in girls. Symptoms include loss of speech, loss of voluntary use of hands, hand-wringing movements, eating problems.

• **Sotos Syndrome**...Causes accelerated growth, enlargement of the skull, facial abnormalities, and often mental retardation. Autistic symptoms may include echolalia, head banging, twirling and spinning, as well as impaired social interaction skills.

• **Tourette Syndrome**...Characterized by involuntary tics such as eye blinking, shrugging, lip smacking, grunting, and cursing. Often present are anxiety attacks and a short attention span.

• **Williams Syndrome**...A rare disorder. Features are often described as "elf-like." Symptoms common to autism include developmental delays in language and gross motor skills, hypersensitivity to sounds, obsession, perseveration with objects, and rocking.

RESOURCES

Association of University Centers on Disabilities (AUCD)
8630 Fenton St, Suite 410
Silver Spring, MD 20910
(301) 588-8252
http://www.aucd.org
A network of university-based and affiliated centers that diagnose and treat individuals with developmental disabilities such as autism.

The Autism Research Centre (ARC)
University of Cambridge
Douglas House, 18b Trumpington Road
Cambridge CB2 2AH, United Kingdom
Telephone: +44 (0)1223 336098/ +44 (0)1223 324661 FAX
http://www.autismresearchcentre.com
The Autism Research Centre was established at the University of Cambridge in 1997 in partnership between the NAS, the University and Lifespan Healthcare NHS Trust. The Center draws together the various strands of research being carried out at Cambridge University.

The Autism Research Foundation (TARF)
c/o Moss-Rosene Lab, W701
715 Albany Street
Boston, MA 02118
(617) 414-7012/(617) 414-7207 FAX
http://www.ladders.org/tarf/
Involved in the research of brain abnormalities in deceased individuals with autism. Sells a videotape about this research, titled "Autism...Challenges and Hope" (members of the Autism Society of America, $16; other, $25). The Autism Research Foundation is not an information center for parents.

Autism Research Institute (ARI)

4182 Adams Av
San Diego, CA 92116
(619) 281-7165
http://www.autism.com/ari

Bernard Rimland, Director. Provides questionnaires used in research on diagnoses of autism in children (Forms E2 and E3). Single copies free. Publishes *Autism Research Review International*, a newsletter reporting the latest research on diagnosis and other aspects of autism.

Autism Society of America (ASA)

7910 Woodmont Av, Suite 300
Bethesda, MD 20814
(301) 657-0881/(800) 3AUTISM
http://www.autism-society.org/

Provides information on the diagnosis of autism. Publishes *The Advocate*, a quarterly newsletter on autism. Coordinates a network of affiliated local chapters.

Cure Autism Now (CAN)

5455 Wilshire Blvd, Suite 715
Los Angeles, CA 90036
(888) 8AUTISM/(323) 549-0547 FAX
http://www.canfoundation.org

Portia Iversen, Director. An organization founded by parents who are dedicated to finding effective biological treatments and a cure for autism. CAN's mission is to fund medical research with direct clinical applications in the field of autism. CAN's Scientific Work Group is made up of top researchers and clinicians, many of whom are parents of children with autism. CAN believes that it is the parents who will mobilize the scientific and medical communities into action.

M.I.N.D. Institute
UC Davis Medical Center
4860 Y St, Room 3020
Sacramento, CA 95817
(888) 883-0961
http://mindinstitute.ucdmc.ucdavis.edu
The objective of the M.I.N.D. Institute is to discover the causes, develop effective treatments and ultimately find a cure for neurodevelopmental disorders.

National Alliance for Autism Research (NAAR)
99 Wall St
Research Park
Princeton, NJ 08540
(888) 777-NAAR
http://www.naar.org
Karen London, President. Founded by parents of children with autism, NAAR's mission is to encourage, promote, support, and fund biomedical research into the causes, prevention, treatment, and cure of the autistic spectrum disorders.

The National Autistic Society (NAS) UK
393 City Rd
London, EC1V 1NG, United Kingdom
+44 (0)20 7833 2299; +44 (0)20 7833 9666 FAX
http://www.nas.org.uk
Provides information and referral services concerning autism in the UK. The NAS website is an excellent source for links to autism groups throughout the world.

Related Disorders:

Asperger's Syndrome Coalition of the United States, Inc. (ASC-US)
PO Box 351268

Jacksonville, FL 32235
(866) 4ASPRGR
http://www.asperger.org
A national nonprofit organization committed to providing the most up-to-date and comprehensive information on Asperger's Syndrome and related conditions.

CANDLE
4414 McCampbell Dr
Montgomery, AL 36106
Jane Rudick, Director. Disseminates information about Landau-Kleffner Syndrome and its treatment. Offers information packet for $5.00.

Epilepsy Foundation
4351 Garden City Dr
Landover, MD 20785
(800) 332-1000/(301) 459-3700
http://www.efa.org
The Epilepsy Foundation is a national, charitable organization, founded in 1968. The only such organization wholly dedicated to the welfare of people with epilepsy, the foundation works for children and adults affected by seizures through research, education, advocacy, and service.

First Signs
PO Box 358
Merrimac, MA 01860
(978) 346-4380/(978) 346-4638 FAX
http://www.firstsigns.org
First Signs is a national non-profit organization dedicated to educating parents and physicians about the early warning signs of autism and other developmental disorders.

Friends of Landau Kleffner Syndrome (FOLKS)
PO Box 749 Erith Kent
DA8 3UA, United Kingdom
+44 1582 411143 (from outside UK) / 01582 411 143 (from
within UK) or 0870 8470707 (UK only)
http://www.bobjanet.demon.co.uk/lks/folks.html
Vicki Horsewell, Founder. Seeks to support families of children with rare conditions such as Landau Kleffner Syndrome
by putting them in touch with other similarly affected families.

International Rett Syndrome Association
9121 Piscataway Rd
Clinton, MD 20735
(800) 818-RETT/(301) 856-3336 FAX
http://www.rettsyndrome.org/
Provides information and support on Rett Syndrome.

National Fragile-X Foundation
P.O. Box 190488
San Francisco, CA 94119
(800) 688-8765/(925) 938-9315 FAX
http://www.nfxf.org
Provides information and support about Fragile X
Syndrome.

Tourette Syndrome Association (TSA)
42-40 Bell Boulevard
Bayside, NY 11361-2820
(718) 224-2999/(718) 279-9596 FAX
http://tsa.mgh.harvard.edu/
Provides information and support services for those with
Tourette Syndrome.

Tuberous Sclerosis Alliance (TSA)
801 Roeder Rd, Suite 750
Silver Spring, MD 20910

(800) 225-6872 (301) 562-9870 FAX
http://www.tsalliance.org
The National Tuberous Sclerosis Association (NTSA) is a nonprofit organization which provides support to people with tuberous sclerosis and their families, awards grants to researchers, and offers education to the public and professional communities. The website will provide links to other societies outside the US.

SUGGESTED READING

Allen, J., S. Baron-Cohen, and C. Gillberg. "Can autism be detected at 18 months? The needle, the haystack, and the CHAT," *British Journal of Psychiatry*, vol. 161, 1992, pp. 839-43. [Reviewed in *Autism Research Review International*, vol. 7, no. 1, 1993, p. 1.]

Attwood, Tony. *Asperger's Syndrome.* London: Jessica Kingsley Publishers, 1998.

Baird, G., T. Charman, S. Baron-Cohen, A. Cox, J. Swettenham, S. Wheelright, A. Drew, and L. Kemal. "A screening instrument for autism at 18 months of age: A six-year follow-up study." *Journal of the American Academy of Child and Adolescent Psychiatry*, vol. 39, p. 694-702, 2000.

Baird, G., S. Baron-Cohen, M. Bohman, M. Coleman, U. Frith, C. Gillberg, P. Howlin, G. Mesibov, T. Peters, E. Ritvo, S. Steffenburg, D. Taylor, L. Waterhouse, L. Wing, and M. Zapella, "Autism is not necessarily a pervasive developmental disorder" (letter), *Developmental Medicine*, vol. 33, no. 4, April, 1991, pp. 363-64. [Reviewed in *Autism Research Review International*, vol. 5, no. 2, 1991, p. 2.]

Baron-Cohen, Simon. *Mind Blindness: An Essay on Autism and Theory of Mind.* Cambridge, MA: MIT Press, 1995.

Blake, Allison. "Asperger's Syndrome: Is it autism?" *Autism Research Review International,* vol. 2, no. 4, 1988, pp. 1, 7.

Bauman, Margaret L., Thomas L. Kemper [eds.] *The Neurobiology of Autism.* Johns Hopkins University Press, 1997.

Fling, Echo R. *Eating an Artichoke : A Mother's Perspective on Asperger Syndrome.* London: Jessica Kingsley Publishers, 2000.

Frith, Uta [ed.]. *Autism and Asperger Syndrome.* Cambridge, NY: Cambridge University Press, 1991.

———. *Autism, Explaining the Enigma.* Cambridge, MA: Basil Blackwell, 1989.

Gillberg, Christopher. *The Biology of the Autistic Syndromes,* 3rd edition. Cambridge; NY: Cambridge University Press. 2000.

Hamilton, Lynn M. *Facing Autism : Giving Parents Reasons for Hope and Guidance for Help.* Colorado Springs, CO: Waterbrook Press. 2000.

Howlin, Patricia. *Children With Autism and Asperger Syndrome: A Guide for Practitioners and Carers.* John Willey and Sons, 1999.

Klin, Ami, F. Volkmar, S. Sparrow [eds.] *Asperger Syndrome.* Guillford Press, 2000.

Lord, Catherine and Risi, Susan. "Early diagnosis in children with autism spectrum disorders." *The Advocate,* vol. 33, no. 4, p23-6, 2000.

Powers, Michael D. [ed.]. *Children With Autism: A Parent's Guide,* 2nd edition. Rockville, MD: Woodbine House, 2000.

Rimland, Bernard. *Infantile Autism: The Syndrome and Its Implications for a Neural Theory of Behavior.* New York:

Appleton Crofts, 1964. (Available through the Autism Research Institute.)

Schopler, Eric, and Gary Mesibov. *Diagnosis and Assessment in Autism*. New York: Plenum Press, 1988.

Schopler, E., R. Reichler, B.R. Renner. "Childhood Autism Rating Scale." (Available from Western Psychological Services, 12031 Wilshire Blvd, Los Angeles, CA 90025.)

Waltz, Mitzi. *Pervasive Developmental Disorders: Finding a Diagnosis and Getting Help*. Arlington, TX: Future Horizons, Inc., 2003.

Willey, Liane Holliday, *Pretending to be Normal: Living with Asperger's Syndrome*. London: Jessica Kingsley Publishers, 1999.

Videos

Attwood, Tony, PH.D. "Asperger's Syndrome." Videotape/DVD. Arlington, TX: Future Horizons, Inc., 1999/2003.

Tests

It is important to discover if there are underlying physical problems for the child diagnosed with autism. In the past, children who have been diagnosed with autism were not given extensive laboratory work-ups. However, many, if not the majority of individuals with autism have underlying physical problems. Also, other disorders have been known to occur along with autism (Fragile-X Syndrome, Moebius Syndrome, William's Syndrome, to name a few). There are also many neurobiological factors that are associated with autism. These include, but are not limited to, epilepsy, tuberous sclerosis, neurofibromatosis, and developmental delay. The book, *The Biology of the Autistic Syndrome* (3rd edition by Christopher Gillberg), is an in-depth reference guide for those wishing to delve deeply into this subject. Below is a basic list of procedures as part of a diagnostic work-up for autism presented by Dr. Gillberg at an Autism Society of America Conference.

1. A complete, detailed family history, looking for genetic abnormalities among family members. **History of the pregnancy, and child's medical history.**

2. Comprehensive, age-appropriate physical, medical, and neurodevelopmental examinations of the child.

3. Laboratory tests:

• **Chromosomal analysis**…with special regard to Fragile-X syndrome.

• **CAT-scan/or MRI scan**…looking for tuberous sclerosis, neurofibromatosis, hypomelanosis of Ito.

• **CSF-protein scan (cerebral spinal fluid)**…for aminoacids, particularly phenylalanine, and CSF monoamines and endorphins.

• **EEG**…for epilepsy, brain damage.

• **Auditory brain stem response**…some children with such a dysfunction cannot tolerate music.

• **Hearing test.**

• **Complete vision exam**…at an early age, for if glasses are required, they would be more easily tolerated.

• **24-hour urinalysis**…including a metabolic screen, that checks for levels of uric acid and calcium.

• **Blood work-up**…for phenylalanine, uric acid, lactic acid, pyruvic acid, and a herpes titer.

The Autism Research Institute publishes a report titled, "Biomedical Assessment Options for Children with Autism and Related Problems," also known as the Defeat Autism Now (DAN!) Protocol. The DAN! Protocol represents a "joining of the minds" of many of the top researchers and physicians in the field. This publication is invaluable to parents and physicians. The DAN! Protocol serves as a guide for doctors and parents seeking to pinpoint the specific metabolic errors in children with autism. This protocol is available from the Autism Research Institute in San Diego, California.

Some of the tests covered in the DAN! Protocol:
- Urinary Peptides
- Organic Acids
- Gluten Sensitivity
- Stool Analysis
- Bowel Permeability
- Secretory IgA
- Liver detoxification
- Amino Acid Analysis
- Folic Acid/Methylmalonic Acid
- Minerals
- Erythrocyte Glutathione Peroxidase Activity
- Food Allergies
- Immunological Tests
- Genetic Tests

RESOURCES

Autism Research Institute (ARI)
4182 Adams Av
San Diego, CA 92116
(619) 281-7165
www.autism.com/ari
Publishes the DAN! Protocol, which is updated periodically. Available for $25. An invaluable resource for

parents and physicians alike. ARI also provides an extensive referral list of physicians who have attended DAN! conferences. There is no charge for lists of three states, $10 for an entire list.

Great Plains Laboratory
11813 West 77th
Lenexa, KS 66214
(913) 341-8949/ (913) 341-6207 FAX
http://www.greatplainslaboratory.com
Dr. William Shaw, Director. Provides a variety of home test kits.

Great Smokies Diagnostic Laboratory
63 Zillicoa St
Asheville, NC 28801
(800) 522-4762
http://www.gsdl.com/
Provides a detoxification profile kit among many other laboratory tests.

Immuno Laboratories
1620 W Oakland Park Blvd
Ft. Lauderdale, FL 33311
(888) 432-8837
http://www.immunolabs.com
Dr. John Rebello, Director. A state, federal, and Medicare-licensed laboratory, Immuno offers comprehensive diagnostic programs in the fields of allergy, immunology, and nutrition.

SUGGESTED READING

Baker, Sidney, and Jon Pangborn. "Biological Assessment Options for Children with Autism and Related Disorders." (DAN! Protocol.) Available for $25 from the Autism Research Institute. See Resource section above.

Caramagno, Liz. "A Diagnostic work-up for autism," *The Advocate*, vol. 24, no. 1, 1992, pp. 13-14. (Summary of a 1990 Gillberg presentation to the Autism Society of America.)

Gillberg, Christopher. *The Biology of the Autistic Syndromes: Clinics in Developmental Medicine, 3rd edition.* Cambridge: Cambridge University Press, 2000.

McCandless, Jacquelyn. *Children with Starving Brains: A Medical Treatment Guide for Autism Spectrum Disorders.* 2nd Ed. Bramble Co, 2003.

Shaw, William. *Biological Treatments for Autism and PDD.* Overland Park, Kansas: Self-published. 1998.

Education

As with all children, educating the person with autism is a challenge! Part of this challenge stems from the fact that autism presents itself in so many different ways. Some children have remarkable skills, some are labeled retarded, some express themselves in aggressive ways, some are content to rock away in a world of their own. The population of individuals with autism holds to no set pattern of behavior. Each child presents his or her own unique behaviors and personality. Yet children with autism can be educated and have the legal right to be. Children with autism need a program that can provide individually appropriate instruction, social interaction, and development, as well as support and respect.

Federal Law in the United States

In the past, parents were given few options regarding the education of their child with disabilities. Often, parents were advised to put their child in an institution and "move on" with their lives. Some parents were able to afford private schools, in which their child had a better chance of receiving some stimulation and personal help. Others were not so fortunate. Today, options have greatly expanded. Now, in the United States, children with disabilities are guaranteed a free public education, thanks to pioneering parents and advocates who pushed the passage of The Education for All Handicapped Act (EHA) of 1975 (better known as Public Law 94-142). This law was updated in 1990, and it is now known as The Individuals With Disabilities Education Act (IDEA, Public Law 101-476).

Under the updated federal law, autism is categorized as a disability in its own right, and individuals with autism are now, specifically, entitled to receive an appropriate education. Under the law, states that provide a special education program meeting federal standards are granted funding from the federal government. The IDEA does not guarantee that a child will be educated in an ideal environment. The law only sets minimum requirements that states must comply with in order to receive funding. Consequently, the quality of special education services varies greatly from state to state.

The law mandates that children with disabilities are entitled to **special education and related services**. Special education means that the instruction afforded the child must be designed to meet the unique needs of each child. Instruction might take place in a classroom, home setting, private school, hospital, or institution. In other words, the child is entitled to receive an education in the environment that is most appropriate for him or her. Children also have the right to be educated in the **least restrictive environment**. That is, they are entitled to be educated with children who are not handicapped. It is up to the parents and school staff to determine how much inclusion or "mainstreaming" is possible for each individual child. Inclusion refers to the amount of time a child with a disability is educated with children without disabilities.

Currently, there is much debate among parents and educators about the topic of inclusion. There is a growing movement that we, as a society, should be moving toward full inclusion. Proponents of full inclusion feel services and education should integrate everyone regardless of the handicapping condition. However, there are just as many parents and educators who feel that this idea, though noble, would simply not be realistic or appropriate for some children. Again, parents, school staff, and others must work together to determine the programs and placements that best fit the unique needs of the child.

Related services are services provided by the school district that are needed for the child to benefit from the special education program. These services may include, but are not limited to, transportation, speech therapy, audiology, occupational or physical therapy, vision services, vocational services, individual instructional assistants, special equipment, and more.

Under the law, each child must have an **Individualized Education Program (IEP)**. The IEP is a written plan which must be in effect 30 days after a child has been evaluated and determined eligible for special education services. This plan is a blueprint for the educational services the child is to receive during the school year. It is developed according to the unique needs of the child, and it is updated at least yearly. The IEP is developed by a team and must include parental involvement as well as representation from the school district (teachers, administrators, school psychologist, speech therapist, etc.). Parents may call an IEP meeting at any time if they are not satisfied with their child's program or progress or if they wish to make changes in the goals and objectives of the plan. According to the Oregon Advocacy Center, the IEP must include:

• present level of performance (a statement of what the child can do); [Author's note: This includes different areas, such as gross and fine motor skills, communication skills, cognitive skills, etc.]

• a statement of annual goals and short-term objectives;

• a statement of the special education and related services to be provided, including the amount of time and description of each related service;

• a statement of the extent the child will participate in regular educational programs (with children without disabilities) and any modifications of those programs needed to permit the child to participate;

• the date special education and related services will begin and how long these services are expected to continue;

• criteria, evaluation procedures and schedules for determining (at least once a year) whether the short-term objectives are met;

• a statement of needed services for transition to community living and employment for all students 16 and older, and for younger students when appropriate. [Broadhurst et al., 1991, p. 8.]

Parents and their children with disabilities now have many rights, but they must become aware of what those rights are and how to exercise them. Parents should become aware of what services their school districts provide. Parents often need to challenge their school districts to improve the quality of services provided. Parents can attend workshops on the legal aspects of special education, get in touch with advocacy groups, join a local chapter of the Autism Society of America, and ask anybody and everybody questions. Read the law, and learn how to quote it when necessary. Slowly but surely, one can gain confidence advocating for a child with a disability.

Early Intervention/Teaching Strategies

One thing most professionals do agree upon is how critical early intervention is for children with autism and other disabilities. It appears that intensive intervention at an early age increases the chances of "normal functioning" for some children with autism. In 1986, The Education of the Handicapped Amendments (Public Law 99-457) mandated early intervention services. Many states have begun early intervention services for children from birth to age three. Under the law, children ages three to five must be provided with the same services the school district provides for older children who qualify for special education services.

An **Individual Family Services Plan (IFSP)** is similar to an Individual Education Plan (IEP) but is designed for the child who qualifies for early intervention services. The IFSP is generally broader in scope than an IEP, including services for the family, such as home consultations, family training, case management services, speech or physical therapy, and classroom options. Early intervention may include help with language skills, social skills, cognitive skills, and/or behavior problems. The purpose of these programs is to reduce the effects of handicaps that may hinder development in small children. Early intervention can occur in any number of settings: at home, in schools, or in centers specializing in the treatment of autism, or in a combination of settings. Since all individuals with autism are unique and need specific teaching, programs for teaching each one should be unique. Parents should understand the philosophy of a program they are considering for their child and feel comfortable with it.

The New Jersey Center for Outreach and Services for the Autism Community, Inc. (COSAC) has developed an excellent set of guidelines for programs designed to educate individuals with autism. They are reprinted here, with permission, from COSAC's handbook, "Autism: Basic Information":

A SUMMARY OF PROGRAMMATIC REQUIREMENTS FOR INDIVIDUALS WITH AUTISM

• **Early diagnosis and appropriate intervention** are vital to the development of individuals with autism.

• **Highly structured, skill-oriented teaching and treatment programs** (programs which simultaneously address skill deficits and problem behaviors by utilizing both skill building and behavior reduction techniques throughout the day), based upon the principles of applied behavior analysis, are the most effective in improving the skills and behavior of individuals with autism.

• **Programs must be tailored to the specific needs of the individual** and delivered in a comprehensive, consistent, systematic, and coordinated manner. Since many children and adults with autism have deficits in many skill areas, providing comprehensive instruction is necessary.

• **Programs should be data-based.** Behaviors should be operationally defined. Teaching and treatment procedures should be outlined. The occurrence of behavior should be recorded before (baseline), during, and after (follow-up) the implementation of teaching and treatment procedures. A summary (i.e., graphs, charts) of data should be provided. Data-based programs permit objective evaluation of the effects of the intervention. On the basis of these data, programs should be revised as needed to assure continued progress.

• **Programs should use individualized motivational systems** (i.e., primary systems [food], token systems, behavior contracts, etc.) and appropriate reinforcement schedules (i.e., continuous, fixed ration, etc.). Motivational systems are based upon the learning principle that individuals tend to repeat or increase behaviors which are followed by positive consequences.

• **Teaching areas should be structured, organized, and distraction-free environments which incorporate intensive one-to-one and small group sessions. Schedules of routines and activities should proceed smoothly and reliably with and across days. Time spent "waiting" should be kept to a minimum.** Classrooms should be equipped with one-way mirrors for observation. For those individuals ready for transition to other settings, larger group sessions ("normal") classrooms should be provided.

• **To provide the consistency necessary for generalization** and maintenance of skills and appropriate behavior.

• Programs should be offered on a **full-day, year-round basis** from preschool through adulthood.

• **Individuals should be taught in multiple settings**, by multiple therapists using a variety of stimuli.

• **A comprehensive home programming/parent training program** should be provided to foster coordination of day and evening programming. Parents should be provided with support groups and extensive in-home behavior management training, which also gives parents a method of coping with many of the child's behavior problems.

• All personnel involved with individuals with autism should be extensively, specifically **trained and continuously evaluated**. On-going skill-based staff training and evaluation are necessary to help ensure staff excellence.

Education is a life-long process. For children with autism, education is critical and should begin as early as possible in a highly-structured, well-designed program. Parents must choose carefully the type of program that will best suit the needs of their child. Finally, parents and teachers must work together to provide a positive, supportive, and consistent learning environment for the individual with autism.

Applied Behavioral Analysis (ABA)

O. Ivar Lovaas and his team at the University of California at Los Angeles published a report documenting their successful treatment of autism with a highly structured behavior modification program for three-year olds. After two years of treatment, 42% of the subjects in an experimental group made major gains in intellectual and social development, and 47% of the children were mainstreamed successfully and were considered to be "indistinguishable from average children on tests of intelligence and adaptive behavior." [See McEachin et al.] Also, the book *Let Me Hear Your Voice*, by Catherine

Maurice, is a well-documented account of one family's experience with the Lovaas method and of how this treatment successfully helped two of their children recover from autism.

Behavior management, or applied behavior analysis, refers to a method of teaching individuals with disabilities, including those with autism. Applied behavior analysis can be an effective teaching technique in many ways. It is not only a strategy that focuses on changing undesirable behaviors; it is also a technique for teaching tasks or skills. For instance, a desired skill might be analyzed and divided into smaller parts. These parts might be taught to an individual slowly, using reinforcers until the skill is learned. Parts of skills may be learned separately and then chained together. Behavioral programs should strive to integrate strategies for teaching new skills and managing behaviors considered problematic because skills and behaviors interact and influence each other.

First, behaviors are observed and analyzed. Then strategies for changing the behavior are attempted and results are monitored to see if the approach is effective. Some programs focus primarily on positive reinforcements ("nonaversives," such as praise or rewards) when the desired behavior is observed. Other programs incorporate punishment ("aversives") as well as positive reinforcers to minimize problem behaviors.

Today, ABA educators almost universally use positive reinforcers without relying on aversives. There has been tremendous change in this field as methods are refined. Terms such as "nonaversive behavior management" and "positive behavior support" are seen throughout ABA literature. [See Horner et al.]

Families for Early Autism Treatment (FEAT) is a well-organized group of parents interested in using ABA techniques for their children with autism. FEAT runs an excellent online newsgroup which offers up-to-date articles and information concerning autism. (See Resources.)

Discrete Trial Training

Discrete trial training is one technique used in ABA or other behavioral programs. A discrete trial is a very specific teaching unit, which usually occurs in a one-on-one setting. The teacher breaks down a task into small parts, teaching each part systematically. Discrete trials include three main components: a cue, a response, and a reinforcer. This sequence is repeated until the child consistently responds correctly. The teacher may initially help the child respond correctly by physically assisting the child in completing the task.

Pivotal Response Training

This technique is also based on ABA principles. However, the teaching tends to be conducted in a more natural setting than traditional ABA. Teachers focus on finding opportunities, or natural reinforcers, to teach desired lessons during typical school or family routines. For instance, a child who requests help opening a door is rewarded by being able to go outside. [See Janzen, p. 75.]

Picture Exchange Communication System (PECS)

This system is also based on the ABA discrete trial teaching format. It was designed to develop communication skills in a context of appropriate activities which interest the child. For example, if the child reaches for an item, such as a glass of juice, he or she is prompted to place a picture of the item in the teacher's hand. The teacher receives the picture and responds with, "You want juice. Here it is!" Thus, the child receives a natural reinforcer and learns that communication is a powerful and effective way to get his or her needs met. [See Bondy and Frost.]

Structured Teaching

Developed by Eric Schopler, Gary Mesibov and others at the TEACCH program in North Carolina (See Resources), structured teaching seeks to improve an individual's skills in a structured educational environment. Home or school environments are modified to better accommodate the needs of the individual with autism. For instance, visual aids or cues are modifications that may help those with autism better understand schedules, transitions, and expectations. This structure reduces anxiety and uncertainties for the individual with autism and allows them to complete tasks independently. Learning to work independently is a goal of this system and can be applied to a variety of activities and settings. Many schools have effectively incorporated strategies designed by the TEACCH program into classrooms where children with autism are taught, and parents often carry similar strategies into the home setting. The TEACCH program provides in-service training for parents and teachers worldwide.

Other Teaching Strategies

Social Stories

Developed by educator Carol Gray, "social stories" are used primarily to teach children how to respond appropriately to a given situation. Social stories are short narratives written in a posititive manner. They are simple and can be repeated as often as neccessary to help a child integrate expectations. Increasing social and communication skills while reducing problem behaviors are the main goals of this approach. For instance, if it is noted that a child tends to wander away from his parents at the mall, a social story might be written featuring the child at the mall, staying close to his parents, followed with a statement about how good the parents feel about this. Social stories often include information that helps children increase their understanding of other people's thoughts and feelings, which are particularly difficult concepts for most children with autism to grasp. [See Gray.]

FastForword

FastForword is a computer CD program developed by Scientific Learning Corporation to help people with reading and language processing disorders.The emphasis is on teaching the brain to discriminate among different sounds. During one clinical trial, children with autism and pervasive development disorders more than doubled their auditory performance over a period of only eight weeks using this system. The software is only available to clinicians, but parents can take a training course if they want to become official providers of the program. [See Scientific Learning Corporation under Resources.]

Earobics

Earobics is an auditory educational program from Cognitive Concepts Inc. This program is less expensive than the FastForword program and can be purchased for home use. The hallmark of the program is teaching listening skills that help children improve language skills. The program consists of six listening games covering up to 114 levels increasing in difficulty. It is believed to be particularly helpful for those struggling with phonics and auditory processing difficulties.

The field of education is ever changing. There are many theories on how best to educate children with autism, and undoubtedly educators will continue to refine methods, integrating the best components from various programs. Educational programs must be chosen with care. Parents will need to gather as much information as they can when choosing the best options for their child. Parents can check with their school district's special education department for a list of programs that may be appropriate for their child. The organizations listed at the end of this chapter offer excellent information and referral services.

Many books have been written about possible techniques for teaching children with autism, who can be especially difficult to educate. For information on the many bookstores that specialize in autism, please refer to the Appendix section of this book.

RESOURCES

Autism Research Institute (ARI)
4182 Adams Av
San Diego, CA 92116
(619) 281-7165
Bernard Rimland, Director. Maintains referral lists of schools and other facilities for children and adults with autism. Provides information and publications on a wide variety of subjects concerning autism. Publishes the *Autism Research Review International*, a quarterly newsletter reporting on the latest research in the field of autism.

Autism Society of America (ASA)
7910 Woodmont Av, Suite 300
Bethesda, MD 20814
(301) 657-0881/(800) 3AUTISM
http://www.autism-society.org
Contact for information about support groups in your lo-
cale. The ASA Information and Referral Service is a
clearinghouse for information about autism, and services
for those with autism. Publishes quarterly newsletter, *The
Advocate*.

Burger School for the Autistic
30922 Beechwood
Garden City, MI 48135
(734) 762-8420
The largest school program in the nation specializing in
the education of children with autism, operating since
1973. Has developed guides for teachers covering curriculum, behavior management, classroom structures, and
more. Free brochure.

Cognitive Concepts Inc. (Earobics)
990 Grove Street
Evanston, IL 60201
(888) 328-8199/ 847-328-5881 FAX
 http://www. cogcon.com
A provider of language and literacy software, books,
Internet services and staff development. Specialize in integrating technology with scientific principles and proven
instructional methods to offer effective and affordable
learning solutions for educators, specialists, and families.

The Eden Family of Services
One Eden Way
Princeton, NJ 08540
(609) 987-0099/(609) 987-0243 FAX

http://www.edenservices.org
The Eden Family of Services includes a 12-month family-oriented school, group homes, employment opportunities, consultation and evaluation services as well as professional training workshops.

Families for Early Autism Treatment (FEAT)
P.O. Box 255722
Sacramento, CA 95865-5722
(916) 843-1536 voice-mail
http://www.feat.org
A nonprofit organization of parents and professionals, designed to help families with children who have received the diagnosis of Autism or Pervasive Developmental Disorder (PDD NOS). FEAT offers a network of support where families can meet each other and discuss issues surrounding autism and treatment options. Offers an excellent autism newsgroup service.

The Handle Institute
1530 Eastlake Avenue E, Suite 100
Seattle, WA 98102
(206) 860-2665/(206) 860-3505 FAX
http://www.handle.org
Organization dedicated to non-drug approaches to a number of neurological disorders including autism. The institute offers clinical services, community information and professional training programs.

Indiana Resource Center for Autism (IRCA)
Institute for the Study of Developmental Disabilities
Indiana University
2853 E 10th St
Bloomington, IN 47408-2601
(812) 855-6508
http://www.isdd.indiana.edu/~irca/

Offers many excellent materials in print and video. Continually revises and updates resource materials for teachers, parents, and service providers. Write for a complete list of titles and costs.

Judevine Center for Autism
1101 Olivette Executive Parkway
St. Louis, MO 63132
(314) 849-4440/(314) 849-2721 FAX
http://www.judevine.org
Offers a three-week training program for parents and professionals wanting to learn the Judevine Method for working with children with autism. Information packet on request.

Lovaas Institute for Early Intervention
Los Angeles Office
11500 West Olympic Blvd., Suite 460
Los Angeles, CA 90064
(310) 914-5433/(310) 914-5463 FAX
www.lovaas.com
Executive Director: Ivar O. Lovaas, Ph.D. The Lovaas Institute for Early Intervention is a research based Institute in California that specializes in teaching pre-school aged children with autism, pervasive developmental disorders, and related developmental disabilities.

Project PACE
9725 SW Beaverton Hillsdale Hwy, Suite 230
Beaverton, OR 97005
(503) 643-7015
Dr. Katherine A. Calouri, Director. PACE stands for Personalizing Autistic Children's Education. Provides individualized instruction based on the principles of behavior modification, or applied behavioral analysis. Offers direct intervention, consultations, and workshops nationwide.

Research and Training Center on Positive Behavioral Support
The University of Oregon
RTC Secretary
Specialized Training Program
Eugene, OR 97403-1235
This center is a five-year project organized through the University of Oregon with five other major universities. Detailed list of research reports, review papers, curriculum materials, and books.

Scientific Learning Corporation
300 Frank H. Ogawa Plaza, Suite 500
Oakland, CA 94612-2040
(888) 665-9707/(510) 444-3580
www. scientificlearning.com
Dr. Michail Merzenich and Dr. Paula Tallal, Founders. Scientific Learning's approach teaches language learning impaired children to process speech more efficiently, building skills they need to comprehend and use language more effectively. FastForword, CD-ROM and Internet-based training programs.

TEACCH
The University of North Carolina
310 Medical School Wing E
Chapel Hill, NC 27599-7180
(919) 966-2174
http://www.teachh.com
Dr. Gary Mesibov, Director. TEACCH stands for Treatment and Education of Autistic and Related Communications Handicapped Children. Offers parent and teacher training workshops and outreach services. Call for information.

University of Kansas
Dr. Ann Turnbull
Beach Center on Families and Disability
Haworth Hall, Room 3136
1200 Sunnyside Avenue
Lawrence, KS 66045-7534
(785) 864-7600/(785) 864-7605 FAX
http://www.beachcenter.org
Provides publications catalog regarding behavioral support issues specifically geared toward families. Works in conjunction with the University of Oregon.

Wrightslaw
http://www.wrightslaw.com
Pam and Pete Wright, Directors. A website providing hundreds of articles, cases, newsletters, and resources about special education law and advocacy topics.

SUGGESTED READING

Books

Anderson, Winifred, and Stephen R. Chitwood. *Negotiating the Special Education Maze,* 2nd. ed. Rockville, MD: Woodbine House, 1990.

International Handbook of Behavior Modification and Therapy. New York: Plenum Publishing, 1990.

Berkell, Diane [ed.]. *Autism: Identification , Education, and Treatment*. 365 Broadway, Hillsdale, NJ 07642: Erlbaum Publishers, 1992.

Broadhurst, Mary E., and Suzy Harris. *Special Education: A Guide for Parents and Advocates*. Portland, OR: Oregon Advocacy Center, 1991. (Pamphlet.)

Cohen, Donald J., and Anne M. Donnellan. *Handbook of Autism and Pervasive Developmental Disorders*. New York: John Wiley and Sons, 1987.

Dake, Lorelei, Sabrina K. Freeman, and Isaac Tamir. *Teach Me Language: A Language Manual for Children with Autism, Asperger's Syndrome and Related Developmental Disorders*. 2nd ed. SFK Books, 1997.

Donnellan, Anne. *Classic Readings in Autism*. New York: College Park Press, 1985.

Harris, Sandra L., and Jan S. Handleman [eds.]. *Aversive and Nonaversive Interventions*. New York: Springer Publishing, 1990.

Hodgdon, Linda. *Visual Strategies for Improving Communication*. Troy, MI: QuirkRoberts Publishing, 1997.

Holmes, David L. *Autism Through the Lifespan: The Eden Model*. Rockville, MD: Woodbine House, 1995.

Janzen, Jan. *Understanding the Nature of Autism*. San Antonio, TX: Therapy Skill Builders, 1996.

——. *Autism: Facts and Strategies for Parents*. San Antonio, TX: Therapy Skill Builders, 1999. (800-228-0752)

Koegel, Robert L., and Lynn Kern Koegel [eds.]. *Teaching Children with Autism: Strategies for Initiating Positive Interactions and Improving Learning Opportunities*. Baltimore, MD: Paul H. Brookes Publishing, 1996.

Lovaas, O. Ivar. *Teaching Developmentally Disabled Children: The ME Book*. Austin, TX: Pro-Ed Publishers, 1980.

McClannahan, Lynn E., and Patricia J. Krantz. *Activity Schedules for Children With Autism : Teaching Independent Behavior.* Rockville, MD: Woodbine House, 1999.

Maurice, Catherine. *Let Me Hear Your Voice.* New York: Alfred Knopf, 1993.

Maurice, Catherine, Gina Green, Stephen C. Luce [eds.]. *Behavioral Intervention for Young Children With Autism: A Manual for Parents and Professionals.* Austin, TX: Pro-Ed, 1996.

Moyes, Rebecca. *I Need Help With School!.* Arlington, TX: Future Horizons, Inc., 2003.

Powers, Michael. *Educating Children with Autism: A Guide to Selecting an Appropriate Program.* Rockville, MD: Woodbine House, 1995.

Schopler, Eric. *Parent Survival Manual: A Guide to Crisis Resolution in Autism and Related Developmental Disorders.* New York: Plenum, 1995.

Schopler, Eric, Robert J. Reichler, and Margaret Lansing. *Individualized Assessment and Treatment for Autistic and Developmentally Disabled Children*, vols. 1 & 2. Baltimore, MD: University Park Press, 1980.

Wright, Pam, and Pete Wright. *Wrightslaw: From Emotions to Advocacy - The Special Education Survival Guide.* Hartfield, VA: Harbor House Law Press, 2002.

Articles

Bondy, A., and L.A. Frost. "The Picture Exchange Communication System." *The Advocate.* vol. 30, no. 5, 1998, pp. 7-9. [In Jan Janzen, *Autism: Facts and Strategies for Parents.*]

Gray, C., and J.D. Garand. "Social Stories: Improving responses of students with autism with accurate social information." *Focus on Autistic Behavior,* vol. 8, no. 1, 1993, pp. 1-10.

Horner, Robert H., Glen Dunlap, Robert L. Koegel, Edward G. Carr, Wayne Sailor, Jacki Anderson, Richard W. Albin, and Robert E. O'Neill. "Toward a technology of 'nonaversive' behavioral support," *Journal of the Association for Persons with Severe Handicaps*, vol. 15, no. 3, 1990, pp. 125-32.

Koegel, Lynn K., Robert L. Koegel, Christine Hurley, and William D. Frea. "Improving social skills and disruptive behavior in children with autism through self-management," *Journal of Applied Behavior Analysis*, no. 2, Summer 1992, pp. 341-53.

McEachin, John J., and O. Ivar Lovaas. "Long-term outcome for children with autism who received early intensive behavioral treatment," *American Journal of Mental Retardation*, vol. 97, no. 4, Jan. 1993, pp. 359-91. [Reviewed in *Autism Research Review International,* vol. 7, no. 1, 1993, pp. 1, 6.]

Roland, C.C., G.G. McGee, T.R. Risley, and B. Rimland. "Description of the Tokyo Higashi Program for autistic children," Autism Research Institute Publication #77, 1987.

Simpson, Richard L., and Gary M. Sasso, "Full inclusion of students with autism in general education settings: Values versus science," *Focus on Autistic Behavior*, vol. 7, no. 3, 1992, pp.1-13. [Reviewed in *Autism Research Review International*, vol. 6, no. 4, 1992, p. 1.]

Nutritional Supplements

In the early 1960s, Dr. Bernard Rimland, director of the Autism Research Institute, heard reports from parents of improvements seen in their children after taking certain vitamins. Dr. Rimland and other scientists investigated these claims and developed a vitamin and mineral therapy which is now considered an effective treatment for some individuals with autism. Researchers concluded that large doses of vitamin B6 (pyridoxine), in combination with magnesium and other vitamins and minerals, are an effective treatment for 45-50% of the individuals with autism who try it. Many scientific, double-blind studies verify the effectiveness of this treatment. [See Rimland, Form Letter.]

Rimland continues to be an enthusiastic supporter of the use of nutritional supplements in the treatment of autism. His newsletter, *Autism Research Review International*, is an invaluable resource to keep current on the latest studies conducted on the use of vitamins and supplements for people with autism. This chapter lists a few popular vitamins and supplements but is by no means exhaustive. However, there are many excellent books which cover vitamins, herbs, and supplements and the roles they play in body functions. A further note of caution: "natural" does not necessarily mean safe. While certain vitamins are safe even in high doses, others are not and could cross-react with medications or existing physical conditions. Consulting a well-trained professional before beginning any new substance is prudent.

B6/Magnesium Supplements

Vitamin B6 and magnesium are water soluble and therefore are not stored in body fat. It is important to take vitamin B6 in combination with other vitamins and minerals in order to help metabolize vitamin B6 and magnesium.

Currently, Kirkman Laboratory produces a relatively inexpensive mega-B6/magnesium supplement (Super Nu-Thera®) in both caplet and powder form. Kirkman has also recently formulated a new product called Super Nu-Thera P5P Formula®. Super Nu-Thera P5P tastes better than the older product. The supplements contain no artificial colors, preservatives, starch, or yeast. The Kirkman supplements also provide many other essential vitamins and nutrients, making them superior to B6 and magnesium alone.

The goal of vitamin therapy is to normalize body metabolism and improve behavior. Studies have shown that vitamin B6 helps to normalize brain waves and urine chemistry, control hyperactivity, and improve overall behavior. It may also help in reducing the effects of allergic reactions by strengthening the immune system. Although improvements vary considerably among individuals, other possible improvements from B6 magnesium therapy are:

• speech improvements

• improved sleeping patterns

• lessened irritability

• increased span of attention

• greater desire for learning

• decrease in self-injury and self-stimulation

• overall improvement in general health. [See Rimland Form Letter.]

In some cases behavioral improvements can be seen in a matter of days. However, the vitamins often take 60-90 days to show any effects. Perseverance and consistency by both the parents and their children is required. Dosage is also an important consideration. The Autism Research Institute provides a form letter on B6/magnesium therapy that includes a detailed description of the treatment, a dosage chart, a table of scientific research data, and an extensive bibliography. Reading this report before beginning megavitamin therapy is highly recommended.

Folic Acid

Folic acid is a B vitamin. Folic Acid acts as a coenzyme along with vitamin B-12 and vitamin C in the breakdown or metabolism of proteins and in the synthesis of new proteins. It is necessary for the production of red blood cells and the synthesis of DNA, as well as tissue growth and cell function. It also helps stimulate the formation of digestive acids.

French researcher Jerome Lejeune reported that supplements of about 250 mcg of folic acid per pound of body weight per day brought on major improvement in children with autism. It is suggested that folic acid be taken with vitamin B12 and vitamin C. [See Hamilton, p.166.]

Vitamin A

Findings by Dr. Mary Megson indicate that cod liver oil, a significant source of vitamin A, might bring about marked improvements for individuals with autism, the most noticeable improvement being increased eye contact, but also the ability to socialize and increased language use. [See Rimland, "Promising Therapies. . . ."] Her research led her to find commonalities in the families of her patients with autism. Her findings included: night-blindness in the mother, and abnormal electroretinograms and using peripheral (side) vision rather than central vision.

Cod liver oil contains vitamin A and is more easily absorbed by a damaged intestinal tract. Megson (among a growing number of other researchers) suspect that individuals with autism may have a weakened or impaired gastrointestinal functioning.

Megson also recommends working with your child's doctor before beginning treatment, using only high-grade, well-known brands of cod liver oil, and give only the recommended dosage. She also advises that Bethanechol, a prescription drug which is a digestive aid be given in addition to the cod liver oil.

Fatty Acids

Essential fatty acid deficiency can result in a compromised immune system, hyperactivity, and eczema, among other problems. Tests can be performed which indicate improper pancreatic function and fatty acid absorption levels. Good sources of essential fatty acids are found in evening primrose oil, fish oils, and flaxseed oil.

Vitamin C

According to a double-blind study conducted in 1993, high doses of vitamin C were shown to have beneficial effects on children with autism. [See Rimland, "Vitamin C. . . ."] Vitamin C is heavily concentrated in the brain, playing a crucial role in brain functioning, although the exact role that it plays is not clearly understood. Many studies have shown that vitamin C improves cognition, protects the body against toxins, and fights bacteria and viruses. Most experts suggest using buffered vitamin C (sodium ascorbate) if large doses are taken.

Zinc

Zinc is useful in immune and gastrointestinal functioning, common problems often seen in people with autism. People with celiac disease often have zinc deficiency. Zinc can help lower elevated levels of other minerals, such as lead and copper. It is easiest to absorb in chelated form (zinc aspartate or zinc picolinate).

Dimethylglycine (DMG)

Despite its technical name, Dimethyglycine (DMG) is a food substance. Its chemical make-up resembles that of water soluble vitamins, specifically vitamin B15. DMG does not require a prescription, and it can be purchased at many health food stores. The most common form of DMG is a tiny (125 mg) tablet packaged in foil. The tablet is pleasant tasting and dissolves rapidly in the mouth.

Anecdotal reports from parents giving their child DMG indicate improvements in the areas of speech, eye contact, social behavior, and attention span. A small child may be given half a 125mg tablet per day, with breakfast, for a few days. For a larger child, one tablet a day should be given until results are noted. The amount may be increased to one or two tablets a day for a child and two or three tablets a day for an adult. Occasionally, if too much DMG is given, the child's activity level has been noticed to increase; otherwise, there are no apparent side effects. DMG should be taken in combination with folic acid. [See Rimland, "Dimethylglycine (DMG) in the treatment of autism."]

Trimethylglycine (TMG) and SAMe

Trimethylglycine (TMG) is DMG with one more methyl group. TMG donates one methyl group (it has three, DMG two) that reduces harmful homocysteins and increases beneficial serotonin by stimulating the production of a precursor called SAMe. SAMe acts as a natural antidepressant by increasing the level of serotonin. The remaining two methyls are DMG. TMG is available through Kirkman Laboratory. SAMe, for use as an antidepressant or serotonin booster, can be purchased at most health food stores.

Melatonin

Melatonin is a hormone produced by the pineal gland in the body, which regulates the body's sleep/wake cycles. It may also play an important role in the immune system. Studies show that melatonin supplements, which can be purchased over the counter at most stores, may help individuals who have trouble sleeping. An informative paper on melatonin use for people with autism can be found at: http://www.autism.org/melatonin.html.

RESOURCES

Autism Research Institute (ARI)
4182 Adams Av
San Diego, CA 92116
(619) 281-7165
http://www.autism.com/ari
Bernard Rimland, Director. Has published extensive information on the subject of vitamin supplements in the treatment of autism. Request their publications list. Form 39E deals specifically with B6/magnesium therapy. Publishes *Autism Research Review International.*

HRI Pfeiffer Treatment Center
1804 Centre Point Dr, Suite 102
Naperville, IL 60563
(630) 505-0300
http://www.hriptc.org
An outpatient medical facility specializing in biochemical testing, diagnosis and individualized nutrient therapy for children and adults. Treatment is based on health history,

physical exam, and extensive laboratory analysis. The treatment program consists of vitamins, minerals, and amino acids that are specifically selected and dosed to address the individual's chemical imbalances.

KareMor® International
PO Box 21858
Phoenix, AZ 85036-1858
(800) 582-5273
Offers a variety of Vitamist® spray nutrients. Call for brochure.

Kirkman Sales Co.
PO Box 1009
Wilsonville, OR 97070
(800) 245-8282
http://www.kirkmanlabs.com
Provides a vitamin/mineral supplement (Super Nu Thera®) containing high doses of vitamin B6 and magnesium as well as other essential vitamins and minerals and a variety of other supplements. Kirkman sales will send free samples upon request.

Mary N. Megson, MD
Pediatric and Adolescent Ability Center
Highland II Bldg
7229 Forest Av, Ste. 211
Richmond, VA 23226
(804) 673-9128/ (804) 673-9195 FAX
http://www.megson.com
Conducting research on vitamin A and children with autism.

Wholesale Nutrition
Box 3345
Saratoga, CA 95070
(800) 325-2664
Sells DMG as well as many other vitamins and supplements at excellent prices.

SUGGESTED READING

Books

DeFelice, Karen L. *Enzymes for Autism and other Neurological Conditions.* Purcell Print, 2002

Hamilton, Lynn. *Facing Autism.* Colorado Springs, CO: Waterbrook Press. 2000.

Leklem, J. and R. Reynolds (eds.). *Vitamin B6 Responsive Disorders in Humans.* New York: Alan Liss, 1988.

Rimland, B. *Infantile Autism: The Syndrome and Its Implications for a Neural Theory of Behavior.* New York: Appleton Century Crofts, 1964.

Schopler, E. and G. Mesibov (eds.). *Neurobiological Issues in Autism.* New York: Plenum Press. 1987.

Waltz, Mitzi. *Pervasive Developmental Disorders: Finding a Diagnosis and Getting Help.* Arlington, TX: Future Horizons, Inc., 2003.

Articles

James E. Jan, R. Freeman, and D. Fast. "Mclatonin treatment of sleep-wake cycle disorders in children and adolescents." *Developmental Medicine and Child Neurology*, vol. 41, 1999, pp.491-500. [Reviewed in *Autism Research Review International*, vol. 13, no. 4, 1999, p. 6.]

Martineau, J., C. Barthelemy, and G. Lelord. "Long-term effects of combined B6-magnesium administration in an autistic child." *Biological Psychiatry*, vol. 21, 1986, pp. 511-18.

Megson, Mary. "The Biological Basis for Perceptual Deficits in Autism." [From Megson website: http://www.megson.com] 1999.

——. "Is Autism a G-Alpha Protein Defect Reversible with Natural Vitamin A?" [From Megson website: http://www.megson.com] 1999.

Rimland, Bernard. "Promising therapies revealed at DAN! Conference." *Autism Research Review International.* vol. 14, no. 1, 2000, p. 6.

——. "Vitamin C in the prevention and treatment of autism." *Autism Research Review International.* vol. 12, no. 2, 1998, p. 3.

——. "Dimethylglycine (DMG) in the treatment of autism." Autism Research Institute Publication 110, 1991. Revised, 1996.

——. "Form Letter Regarding High Dosage Vitamin B6 and Magnesium Therapy for Autism and Related Disorders." Autism Research Institute Publication 39, 1991. Revised, 1996.

Biomedical Interventions

No primary medication is used to treat autism. Medications are usually prescribed to decrease specific symptoms associated with autism. These symptoms may include self-injurious behavior, aggressive behavior, seizures, depression, anxiety, hyperactivity, or obsessive-compulsive behavior. Medications alone are not a solution to the problems associated with autism. Individuals with autism need well rounded intervention, including behavior management strategies, environmental modifications, and positive support services. Parents wishing to try medications for their children should be given the support and knowledge necessary to maintain a safe level of treatment. Parents need to be aware of potential risks and harmful side effects, and should carefully weigh them against possible benefits before treatment begins. Dosage should be carefully considered and monitored. There must be good communication between parents, physicians, service providers, and school personnel to monitor treatment with any medication. Accurate data on the effects of medication are also essential. [See Gray, pp. 1-4.]

Medications

Listed below are the various classifications of medications used to treat symptoms associated with autism.

• **Antipsychotics**...Also known as neuroleptics or "major" tranquilizers. Sometimes used to treat severe aggression, self-injurious behavior, agitation, or insomnia. Side effects may include tardive dyskinesia (an involuntary muscular twitching, which may become irreversible), also tremors, stiffness, and sleepiness. Medications include Mellaril™, Haldol™, Thorazine™, Risperdal™.

• **Anticonvulsants**...Given to control seizures. Side effects may include drowsiness, gum swelling, negative behavioral and cognitive performance. Medications include Tegretol™, Depakote™, Dilantin™.

• **Anti-anxiety**...Sometimes prescribed to relieve "nerves," anxiety, or anxiousness. Medications vary in effectiveness for long-term anxiety. Side effects associated with Valium™ and Librium™ may include increased behavior problems. Some antidepressants are used to treat chronic anxiety. They include Trofranil™ and Elavil™.

• **Antidepression, Antimania**...These medications are used to treat disorders such as depression, compulsive behaviors, mania, panic, or anxiety. Lithium™ and Depakote™ are sometimes prescribed for bipolar (manic-depressive) disorder. Anafranil™ and Prozac™ are sometimes prescribed for compulsive behavior. Most antidepressants take two to three weeks before effectiveness is noted. Side effects may include agitation, insomnia, decreased appetite, hyperactivity.

• **Beta Blockers**…These medications are usually used to control blood pressure, but are sometimes given to individuals to decrease aggression or hyperactivity caused by a rush of adrenaline. The beta blockers help to prevent the adrenalin rush and allow the individual to control impulsive reactions. Medications include Inderal™ and Clonidine/Catapres™. May cause drowsiness, irritability, lowered blood pressure.

• **Opiate Blockers**…Some researchers theorize that self-injurious behaviors may cause the brain to release endorphins (chemicals which produce an opiate-like "high"), which may cause the individual to continue the self-injury in order to feel good. Opiate-blockers act to block the pleasurable sensation and allow the individual to feel the pain. As a result, self-injury may diminish. Sometimes, a sedating effect has been noted. Naltrexone/ Trexan™ is an opiate blocker. These drugs may also improve socialization and general well-being.

• **Sedatives**…Given to individuals who have difficulty sleeping. Often medication is gradually withdrawn when normal sleep patterns are established. If the medication is not suitable for an individual it can cause excitation or sleeplessness. Chloral Hydrate™, Noctec™, and Benedryl™ are examples of sedatives.

• **Stimulants**…Sometimes prescribed for hyperactivity and attention or concentration problems. Side effects may include decreased appetite, sadness, tantrums, and hyperactivity after medication wears off. Ritalin™ and Dexedrine™ are stimulants.

Medications can sometimes help an individual with autism by providing relief from specific symptoms that interfere with daily life. Their use should be carefully monitored both by parents and professionals caring for the individual with autism. To find the latest articles on medical treatments, visit Medline, or PubMed (http://www.pubmed.com).

There are other biomedical interventions that have been used with differing of success for the treatment of autistic symptoms, particularly to help the immune system function better. Secretin therapy made national news, and many scientific studies are underway to help determine its effectiveness. IVIG and Transfer Factor are other therapies that show promise, and like most treatments, more studies are needed to fully understand their implications for treating autistic symptoms.

Secretin

Secretin is a hormone and a neurotransmitter that plays a part in digestion. It is a polypeptide composed of 27 amino acids and is secreted by cells in the digestive system. Secretin stimulates the pancreas, which in turn emits digestive fluids rich in bicarbonate that neutralize the acidity of the intestines, stimulate the stomach to produce pepsin (an enzyme that aids in digestion) and stimulate the liver to produce bile. Secretin is also involved with activities in the brain, including stimulating the production and utilization of the neurotransmitter, serotonin. [See Rimland, "The Autism-Secretin . . ."]

Secretin has traditionally been used to test the function of the pancreas and to uncover gastrointestinal disorders. It was in 1996 that Victoria Beck, the mother of a child with autism, noticed that her son showed dramatic improvement after an endoscopy during which a secretin challenge test was performed. Determined to discover the cause of her son's improvement, Beck eventually made the connection to secretin. Beck has documented her work in a short book, *Unlocking the Potential of Secretin,* which is available from the Autism Research Institute. A 1998 study of three children with autism treated with secretin showed positive results. [See Horvath.]

Since then, secretin has been administered to thousands of children. Positive changes reported by some parents from the use of secretin include increased eye contact, normalized bowel movements, increase in social awareness, and improved speech. Short-term negative side effects reported include increased hyperactivity, self-stimulation, and aggression. Most of these negative reactions subside within two weeks. [See Rimland, "Secretin Update. . . ."]

Secretin can be administered by intravenous (IV) infusion, and those who have received more than one infusion noted more positive results. [See Waltz, p. 138.] Other methods of administration have gained popularity, including intramuscular injection, transdermal application, and sublingual drops. Much research is required before physicians can determine exactly how effective these methods are and what the proper dosage might be.

While secretin is considered very safe by some, the use of secretin to treat autism has raised concerns. There is the possibility that antibodies could be produced as a reaction to the porcine (pig) secretin currently used. [See Hamilton, p. 151.] This risk could be minimized as newer synthetic human secretin is developed.

Although secretin has been given to thousands of children, seizure reactions have been reported following secretin infusions in only two children, and one child stopped breathing temporarily. Even enthusiastic support-

ers of secretin recognize the need for caution and awareness of potential harmful reactions. [See Rimland,
"Secretin Update . . . ."] To stay current on secretin
therapy visit the website http://www.secretin.com, or
http://www.autism.com/ari.

IVIG Therapy

Immunoglobulin G (IVIG) is one antibody used by
the immune system to defend against infection. IVIG
therapy has been used to treat immunological disorders
since the early 1980s. It has received attention as a possible treatment for autistic symptoms since children with
autism often demonstrate immune system abnormalities.
As with so many new and experimental treatments, no one
is quite sure how IVIG works in children with autism;
some postulate it might have an anti-inflammatory affect
on the brain or may block the action of autoimmune antibodies.

IVIG is a blood product. In IVIG therapy the patient
receives a transfusion, which takes several hours. In one
study, ten children with autism received a transfusion every six weeks with a total of four treatments. There was
significant improvement observed in one child, slight improvement in four, and no improvement in the five other
children. [See Plioplys, pp. 79-82.]

There are serious concerns about IVIG therapy. Although plasma donors are screened, there is still a risk of
blood-borne infection. Because of the risk of disease
transmission through plasma, IVIG products, even though
monitored, run the risk of carrying traces of viruses and
other diseases. IVIG is costly not covered by most insurance, and can be difficult to obtain.

Transfer Factor

Another therapy which may hold potential for the treatment of immune system dysfunction and therefore may have implications for the treatment of autism is Transfer Factor (TF). Our bodies naturally produce antibodies, which serve to fight off antigens. (Antigens are molecules that are components of disease carriers such as viruses and bacteria.) The production of antibodies in the immune system is known as humoral response.

Transfer Factors are tiny protein molecules that act as "messengers" to our immune system. They also work with our white blood cells in another type of immune response, known as cell-mediated response. This immune-strengthening response can be transferred from one host to another, and it can be done without introducing antibodies. [See Fletcher, pp. 48-9.]

As an example, colostrum, which is contained in breast milk, provides newborns with TFs from the mother, which helps with resistance to infections. Colostrum supplements may be beneficial in treating children with autism because they foster healing of the intestinal lining, help rid the body of unwanted yeast and bacteria, or stimulate the release of serotonin. [See Hamilton, p. 183.] For information on colostrum supplements, contact Kirkman Laboratory. (See Resources.) Kirkman colostrum is a bovine supplement, and some children could have an immune reaction to it. However, it is gluten, lactose, and casein free.

Antigen-specific Transfer Factor, also known as Dialysable Lymphocyte Extract (DLyE), refers to the introduction of specific TFs to combat particular problems. TF products are obtained from host animals that are exposed to specific viruses or bacteria in order to achieve a desired immune response. The goal of introducing the body to these TFs over a period of time is to help our own immune system learn to recognize these antibodies and combat them. Some studies have found antigen-specific Transfer Factors to be useful in treating autistic symptoms. [See Fudenberg.] To determine if this would be an appropriate treatment option to try, work with a qualified professional.

Finally, there is growing interest in this country in the use of "alternative" therapies such as homeopathic medicine. Homeopathic remedies are based on the principle of "like cures like." An extremely minute amount of substance (think of a drop of water in a swimming pool) is introduced sublingually to stimulate the body's own reaction to heal itself. Homeopathy is a fairly mainstream practice in the United Kingdom and other countries. There are some licensed medical doctors who also practice homeopathy. As with any service provider, it is important to find a certified practitioner from an accredited program. See Resource section below for more information on homeopaths in North America.

RESOURCES

Autism Research Institute (ARI)
4182 Adams Av
San Diego, CA 92116
(619)281-7165
http://www.autism.com/ari
Dr. Bernard Rimland, Director. Publishes *Autism Research Review International*, a newsletter which summarizes the latest research on medications used in the treatment of individuals with autism. Can provide a bibli-

ography of reading materials and articles on this subject.

Center for Health and Healing
Beth Israel Medical Center
http://www.healing-arts.org/children
This website, Forum on Alternative and Innovative Therapies, provides much information on alternative medical and physical therapies for the treatment of brain-injured children, including autism.

IVIG Therapy/Dr. Sudhir Gupta
University of California
Medical Sciences I, Room C-240
Irvine, CA 92717
(714)824-5818/ (714)824-4362 FAX
Intravenous Immune Globulin (IVIG) is a therapy used to treat autoimmune disorders and immune deficiency syndromes. Patients must undergo immunologic screening to determine whether treatment is indicated.

The National Alliance for the Mentally Ill (NAMI)
200 N Glebe, Suite 1015
Arlington, VA 22203
(703)524-7600/(800)950-6264
http://nami.org.
An excellent resource for information on new drugs for neurological disorders.

SUGGESTED READING

Books

Gillberg, Christopher [ed.]. *Diagnosis and Treatment of Autism*. New York and London: Plenum Press, 1989.

Hamilton, Lynn. *Facing Autism.* Colorado Springs, CO: Waterbrook Press, 2000.

McCandless, Jacquelyn. *Children with Starving Brains: A Medical Treatment Guide for Autism Spectrum Disorders.* 2nd Ed. Bramble Co, 2003.

Tsai, Luke. *Taking the Mystery out of Medications in Autism/Asperger's Symdrome: A Guide for Parents and non-Medical Professionals.* Arlington, TX: Future Horizons, Inc., 2001.

Waltz, Mitzi. *Pervasive Developmental Disorders: Finding a Diagnosis and Getting Help.* Arlington, TX: Future Horizons, Inc., 2003.

Articles

Gray, Linda. "Medication issues in autism." Indiana Resource Center for Autism Newsletter, vol. 6, no. 2, 1993, pp.1-4.

Grandin, Temple. "New drug treatments for autistic adults and adolescents." *The Advocate*, vol. 23, no. 3, 1991.

——. "Evaluating the Effects of Medication." [Center for the Study of Autism Website Publication, http:www.autism.org, 1998.]

Fletcher, D.J. "Educating the Immune." *Alternative Medicine*, May, 2000, pp. 48-55.

Fudenberg, H. H. "Dialysable Lymphocyte Extract (DLyE) in Infantile Autism: A Pilot Study." *Biotherapy*, vol. 9, 1996, p. 143.

Horvath, K., G. Stefanatos, K. N. Sokolski, R. Wachtel, L. Nabors, & J. T. Tildon. "Improved social and language skills after secretin administration in patients with autistic spectrum disorders." *Journal of the Association for Academic Minority Physicians*, vol. 9, no. 1, 1998, pp. 9-15.

McDougle, C.J., J.P. Holmes, D.C. Carlson, G.H. Pelton, D.J. Cohen, & L.H. Price. "A double-blind, placebo-controlled study of risperidone in adults with autistic disorder and other pervasive developmental disorders." *Archives of General Psychiatry*, vol. 55, no. 7, 1998, pp. 633-41.

Plioplys, Audrius. "Intravenous immunoglobulin treatment of children with autism." *Journal of Child Neurology*, vol. 13, 1998, pp. 79-82.

Rimland, Bernard. "Secretin Update: The Safety Issue." ARRI Website, http://www.autism.com/ari December, 1999.

——. "The Autism-Secretin Connection." *Autism Research Review International*, vol. 12, no. 3, 1998, p. 3.

——. "IVIG therapy tested in autism, Landau-Kleffner syndrome." *Autism Research Review*, vol. 12, no. 2, 1998.

——. "Naltrexone: Opioid blocker still looking good." *Autism Research Review International*, vol. 6, no. 1, 1992, pp. 1-2.

Wing, Lorna. *The Autistic Spectrum: A Guide for Parents and Professionals*. Trans-Atlantic Publications, 1997.

Autism Research Institute
4182 Adams Avenue • San Diego, CA 92116
PARENT RATINGS OF BEHAVIORAL EFFECTS OF DRUGS AND NUTRIENTS

The parents of autistic children represent a vast and important reservoir of information on the benefits—and adverse effects—of the large variety of drugs and other interventions that have been tried with their children. Starting in 1967 the Autism Research Institute has been collecting parent ratings of the usefulness of the many interventions tried on their autistic children.

The following data have been collected from the more than 16,000 parents who have completed our questionnaires designed to collect such information. For the purposes of the present table, the parent responses on a six-point scale have been combined into three categories: "made worse" (ratings 5 and 6), "no effect" (ratings 1 and 2), and "made better" (ratings 3 and 4).

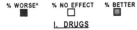
■ % WORSE[A] □ % NO EFFECT ▨ % BETTER

I. DRUGS

Note: Several seizure drugs are listed twice. The first listing (behav) shows their behavioral effects, and the second listing (seiz) shows their effects on seizures.

DRUGS	NO. OF CASES[B]	BETTER/ WORSE[A]
Adderall	33	1.5:1
Amphetamine	990	0.5:1
Anafranil	261	0.9:1
Antibiotics	1357	0.3:1
Antifungals[C]		
Diflucan	28	10.0:1 [D]
Nystatin	384	10.6:1
Atarax	360	0.9:1
Benadryl	2038	1.1:1
Beta Blocker	214	2.2:1
Buspar	145	1.4:1
Chloral Hydrate	257	0.6:1
Clonapin	67	2.5:1
Clonidine	641	2.2:1
Clozapine	37	0.6:1
Cogentin	106	1.5:1
Cylert	492	0.5:1
Deanol	183	2.0:1
Depakene (behav)	601	1.3:1
Depakene (seiz)	419	5.4:1
Desipramine	35	1.5:1
Dilantin (behav)	975	0.8:1
Dilantin (seiz)	317	4.0:1
Felbatol	22	1.3:1 [D]
Fenfluramine	426	1.4:1

DRUGS	NO. OF CASES[B]	BETTER/ WORSE[A]
Haldol	33	1.0:1
Haldol	992	0.9:1
Lithium	299	1.2:1
Luvox	23	2.5:1 [D]
Mellaril	1863	1.3:1
Mysoline (behav)	113	0.3:1
Mysoline (seiz)	42	1.8:1
Naltrexone	157	1.5:1
Paxil	34	2.3:1
Phenergan	168	0.7:1
Phenobarbital (behav)	956	0.7:1
Phenobarbital (seiz)	376	3.0:1
Prolixin	62	1.4:1
Prozac	552	1.1:1
Risperdal	58	4.1:1
Ritalin	2788	0.6:1
Stelazine	393	1.0:1
Tegretol (behav)	1081	1.4:1
Tegretol (seiz)	572	5.9:1
Thorazine	836	0.7:1
Tofranil	535	1.0:1
Valium	695	0.7:1
Zarontin (behav)	97	0.7:1
Zarontin (seiz)	61	2.0:1
Zoloft	69	0.9:1

A. "Worse" refers to behavior. Drugs, but not nutrients, typically also cause physical problems i used long-term.

B. No. of cases is cumulative over several decades, so does not reflect current usage levels (e.g., Haldol is now seldom used).

C. Antifungal drugs are used only if autism is yeast-related.

D. Better/worse ratios marked "D" are unstable du to the small number of cases rated "worse." A small change in "worse" changes the ratio greatly

E. Calcium effects not due to dairy-free diet; statistic similar for milk drinkers and non-milk drinkers.

F. Insufficient data to calculate ratio

II. SUPPLEMENTS

NUTRIENT	NO. OF CASES[B]	BETTER/ WORSE[A]
Calcium[E]	417	19.2:1
Dimethylglycine (DMG)	3217	6.5:1
Folic Acid	579	13.9:1
Magnesium alone	187	4.7:1
Melatonin	38	. [F]
Vitamin B3 (niacin/niacinamide)	255	8.5:1
Vitamin B6 alone	431	4.5:1
Vitamin B6 and magnesium	3582	11.5:1
Vitamin C	637	14.3:1
Zinc	349	11.9:1

Dietary Interventions

The role diet, allergies, and food sensitivities play in the life of a child or adult with autism is gaining more and more attention, particularly as parents document their successes and share information over the Internet and with support groups. Although any food could be an offender, there are several foods that are considered prime suspects in causing behavior disturbances. Working together, parents and researchers continue to refine the methods of dietary intervention and other allergy-targeted treatments to reduce autistic symptoms.

Parents wishing to explore these avenues of treatment must do their homework. Extensive reading is required. Finding a competent professional with whom you feel comfortable may take some time. This may mean finding a doctor who specializes in orthomolecular medicine, a naturopathic physician, or a doctor who has been trained in nutrition. Finally, commitment and perseverance are required to make dietary changes and stick to them. Luckily, there are now many excellent books available on diet, food sensitivities, and allergies.

The 'Leaky Gut' Problem

Some research studies have indicated that individuals with autism may have particular trouble digesting two sources of protein: gluten (found in wheat, rye, oats, and other grains) and casein (protein from milk). In her book, *Unraveling the Mystery of Autism and Pervasive Developmental Disorder,* Karyn Seroussi provides a well-documented account of her quest to help her son, Miles, by eliminating gluten and dairy from his diet. Guidelines for implementing a gluten-free and casein-free diet program can be ordered through the Autism Research Institute.

There is growing evidence that consumption of food products containing gluten (e.g., wheat, barley, oats, rye) and casein (dairy products such as milk, ice cream, yogurt) may lead to alteration of brain chemistry. During the digestion process, proteins, such as gluten and casein, are broken down into smaller chains, called peptides, and these proteins are then broken down further into amino acids. Many people with autism have a 'leaky gut,' small holes in the intestinal tract that may be caused by viral infection in the gut, yeast infection (candida albicans), low levels of phenyl sulfurtransferase, and more.

When a person has a "leaky gut," the peptides may enter the bloodstream instead of remaining in the intestinal tract. These peptides may then cross the blood-brain barrier and can alter brain function–for example, by retarding neural growth. Since peptides from gluten (gluteomorphins) and peptides from casein (casomorphins) have similar biochemical properties similar to those of morphine, their crossing of the blood-brain barrier cause a morphine-like high, cause insensitivity to pain, and more.

Two tests can be used to examine this "leaky gut" and gluten/casein problem. One test, called the Bowel Permeability Study, is used to determine whether the person has a leaky gut, and a Urinary Peptide Test can determine whether there are abnormal peptides in the urine. Several laboratories are currently developing digestive enzyme supplements that may prove beneficial to individuals who have enzymatic deficiency or trouble with gluten and casein digestion. (See Resources, Kirkman Sales.)

Allergies and Sensitivities

In her book, *Fighting For Tony,* author and mother Mary Callahan let the world know about the possible connection of cerebral allergies and autism. Her son, diagnosed with autism, improved dramatically over time after cow's milk was eliminated from his diet. The term "cerebral allergy" refers to the effect a food intolerance may have on the brain. This intolerance may cause the tissues of the brain to swell and become inflamed, much as the nose becomes red and irritated if one is allergic to pollen . . .but in the brain, we cannot see this swelling occur. The symptoms, however, may include disturbances of learning and behavior.

Sugar is another food substance that may cause behavioral disturbances. Not only are some children allergic to it, they may suffer from an inability to metabolize it properly. In this condition, known as "relative hypoglycemia," blood sugar levels drop too fast after a person consumes foods containing simple sugars or simple carbohydrates. Hypoglycemia may also be triggered by an allergic reaction. As a result, the adrenal glands in the body become stressed and depleted, and over time they cease to function normally. The effects of hypoglycemia may include mood swings, irrational behavior, irritability, sleep disturbances, nervousness, and the list goes on.

Other foods that cause allergic reactions are, unfortunately, foods we often consume the most. Wheat is one such food as well as other products that contain gluten. Some children cannot tolerate even the smallest amount of gluten without having their behavior become unmanageable. Milk, as in the case of Tony, has been linked over and over to behavior problems. As discussed earlier, products containing casein may cause particular trouble for individuals with autism. Other common food offenders include corn, chocolate, chicken, tomatoes, and certain fruits. However, any food can cause an intolerance or sensitivity. The key is uncovering the problem foods, and often there may be more than one.

Besides food, other substances may cause reactions in children. Hyperactivity has been linked to an intolerance to food additives, such as phosphates and food colorings. Molds, chemicals, perfumes, and other substances may cause allergic reactions. One treatment, enzyme-potentiated desensitization (EPD), involves giving a very low dose of an allergen in combination with an enzyme. (See Shaw, pp. 115-16.] For more information on this immunotherapy, contact the American EPD Society (See Resources.)

In addition, behavior and learning problems have been linked to the toxicity of heavy metals such as lead and aluminum. A hair-mineral analysis test may be beneficial in revealing heavy metal toxicity or deficiency of essential minerals. If high levels of certain metals or minerals are found, using chelation therapy is one way to remove them from the body.

There are ways to uncover allergies and intolerances.

A good first step is to have urinary peptide tests performed, as well as a test for antibodies, particularly gluten and casein. A common test for allergies is the radioallergosorbent test (RAST), a blood test which measures immunoglobulin E (IgE) antibodies to specific foods. One ELISA test detects increases in immunoglobulins IgE and in IgG antibodies. These antibodies increase in response to fixed and delayed allergies. Your doctor might also feel that a test for celiac disease, a condition in which gluten causes damage to the intestinal lining, is warranted. Physical symptoms indicative of allergies include red cheeks and ears, dark circles under the eyes or redness of the eyes. However, allergies may be present without these symptoms.

Where is the best place to begin? Start by eliminating "junk" foods. Read labels on packaged and processed foods. You may be amazed at how much sugar is added to everything! Start improving your family's diet by serving fresh foods and foods that haven't been refined to the point where virtually all of the nutrients are gone. Also start observing your child. Is there a food he or she craves? Ironically, it is the food most often craved that may be causing allergic reactions. If you decide to begin the gluten-free and casein-free diet, contact ANDI for a wealth of information and support. (See Resources.) Support groups like ANDI and resources from the Internet may help to avoid "hidden" sources of foods that might not be seen on a label. For instance, a conveyor belt in a food factory might be dusted with gluten, and this will not show up on a food label.

Careful research and consultation with a professional who is skilled in this area are probably your best bets in determining which tests are most appropriate. More importantly, food intolerances can often be determined by beginning a rotation or an elimination diet and observing any changes in behavior. This is carried out at home and doesn't cost anything except time and the money for the food. Many of the books listed below discuss exactly how to begin a rotation diet and what sort of changes to look for. If possible, get the help of a professional, one who is *supportive* and *knowledgeable* about how food sensitivities can affect the nervous system.

At first, changes in diet may seem traumatic to everyone in the family. However, if an allergy is uncovered, treatment can be very successful. Approach the diet/allergy connection slowly, read as much as you can, and observe eating patterns in your own family. Try not to become overwhelmed with all the possibilities. Even small changes can sometimes bring significant results.

RESOURCES

Allergy-Induced Autism
11, Larklands
Longthorpe, Peterborough
PE3 6LL, Cambridgeshire
United Kingdom
http://www.autismmedical.com
Rosemary Kessick, Director. Offers dietary information concerning children who may suffer from allergy-induced autism. Currently involved in a research study with Birmingham University (UK) looking for possible enzyme deficiencies in children with autism.

American Academy of Environmental Medicine (AAEM)
7701 E Kellog, Suite 625
Wichita, KS 67207
(316) 684-5500/(316) 684-5709 FAX
http://www.aaem.com
Publishes AAEM Directory of members. Provides educational aids, tapes, and audio-visual presentations on environmental medicine.

American Association of Naturopathic Physicians (AANP)
3201 New Mexico Av NW, Suite 350
Washington, DC 20016
(866) 538-2267/(202) 274-1992 FAX
http://www.naturopathic.org
Can provide a list of associated naturopathic physicians or refer you to a registered naturopathic physician in your area.

American EPD Society
PO Box 31126
Santa Fe, NM 87594-1126
http://epdallergy.com
Provides information for patients, physicians and administrators involved with Enzyme Potentiated Desensitization (EPD) immunotherapy.

Analytical Research Labs
2225 W Alice
Phoenix, AZ 85021
(602) 995-1581
Can provide a hair analysis to check for toxic metals and mineral imbalances.

Antibody Assay Labs
1715 E Wilshire Blvd, Suite 715
Santa Ana, CA 92705
(800) 522-2611
http://www.antibodyassay.com
Offers a multitude of tests including a gluten and casein sensitivity evaluation, ELISA, antibody titers, and more.

Association for Comprehensive NeuroTherapy
PO Box 210848
Royal Palm Beach, FL 33421-0848
(561) 798-0472
http://www.latitudes.org
Links a variety of remedies and practices with a spectrum of disorders that have things in common with autism. Publishes the newsletter, *Latitudes*.

Autism, Intolerance, and Allergy (AIA) a program of:
The Feingold Association of the United States (FAUS)
127 E Main St, #106
Riverhead, NY 11901
(800) 321-3287
http://www.feingold.org
Jean Curtain, Director. AIA is a group of parents and medical professionals dedicated to investigating the biochemical origins of the autistic condition. Provides information on dietary intervention for children and adults with autism.

Autism Network for Dietary Intervention (ANDI)
PO Box 17711
Rochester, NY 14617-0711
(609) 737-8453 FAX
http://www.autismNDI.com
Lisa Lewis and Karen Seroussi, Directors. Offers a newsletter and product catalogue for those interested in dietary

interventions for children with autism and related disorders.

Autism Research Institute
4182 Adams Av
San Diego, CA 92116
(619) 281-7165
http://www.autism.com/ari
Bernard Rimland, Director. Offers many informational packets on diet and nutrition. The DAN! Protocol is an excellent source for information on tests and laboratories.

Autism Research Unit
School of Health Sciences
University of Sunderland
Sunderland SR2 7EE
United Kingdom
(44) 0 191 567 0420
http://www.osiris.sunderland.ac.uk/aut-cgi/homepage
Paul Shattock, researcher at this unit is collecting data from specific types of urinary peptide tests of people with autism.

Celiac Disease Foundation
13251 Ventura Blvd, Suite 1
Studio City, CA 91604-1838
(810) 990-2354/(818) 990-2379 FAX
http://www.celiac.org
Provides services, information, and and support to persons with celiac disease.

Great Plains Laboratory
11813 West 77th
Lenexa, KS 66214
(913)341-8949/(913) 341-6207 FAX
http://www.autism.com/shaw-yeast/
William Shaw, Director. Lab provides home test kits and lab analysis for a variety of autism and related conditions.

Immuno Laboratories
1620 W Oakland Park Blvd
Ft. Lauderdale, FL 33311
(800)231-9197
http://www.immunolabs.com
Dr. John Rebello, Director. A state, federal, and Medicare-licensed laboratory, Immuno offers comprehensive diagnostic programs in the fields of allergy, immunology, and nutrition. Tests include IgG and IgE (food allergy blood tests) as well as a Candida Albicans Assay.

Kirkman Sales Co.
PO Box 1009
Wilsonville, OR 97070
(800) 245-8282
http://www.kirkmanlabs.com
Offers a variety of supplements.

SUGGESTED READING

Books

Baker, S.M., and Pangborn, John. *Biomedical Assessment Options for Children with Autism and Related Problems. The DAN Protocol*. San Diego: CA, 1999, Autism Research Institute Publication.

Callahan, Mary. *Fighting for Tony*. New York: Simon & Schuster, 1987.

Crook, William. *Solving the Puzzle of Your Hard-To-Raise Child*. New York: Random House, 1987. (Available from Pedicenter Press, PO Box 3116, Jackson, TN 38301.)

Crowell, Beth and Andy. *Dietary Intervention as a Therapy in the Treatment of Autism and Related Disorders.* 1992. (Available from Beth and Andy Crowell, 208 South St, PO Box 801, Housatonic, MA 01236. $14.95+S&H.)

Fredericks, Carl. *Psycho-Nutrition.* New York: Grosset and Dunlap, 1976.

Hersey, Jane. *Why Can't My Child Behave?* 1996. (Available from Pear Tree Press, PO Box 30146, Alexandria, VA 22310. $22.00 ppd.)

Lewis, Lisa. S*pecial Diets for Special Kids.* Arlington, TX: Future Horizons, 1998. (800)489-0727.

Mandell, M., and L. Scanlon. *Dr. Mandell's 5-Day Allergy Relief System.* New York: Thomas Y. Crowell, 1979.

Philpott, William H. *Brain Allergies.* New Canaan, CT: Keats Publishing, 1980.

Rapp, Doris. *Is This Your Child?* New York: William Morrow, 1991.

Reichelt, Karl, Ann-Mari Knivsberg, Gunnar Lind, and Magne Nodland. "Probable etiology and possible treatment of childhood autism." *Brain Dysfunction,* no. 4, 1991, pp. 308-19. [Reviewed in *Autism Research Review International,* vol. 7, no. 1, 1993, pp. 4-7.]

Seroussi, Karyn. *Unraveling the Mystery of Autism and Pervasive Developmental Disorder: A Mother's Story of Research and Recovery.* New York: Simon & Schuster, 2000.

Shaw, William. *Biological Treatments for Autism and PDD.* Overland Park, Kansas. Self-Published, 1998.

Articles

Edelson, Stephen M., "Allergies and Food Sensitivities." [Salem, OR. From the Center for the Study of Autism website, http://www.autism.com/csa]

Eufemia, P. D., et al. "Abnormal Intestinal Permeability in Children with Autism," *Acta Paediatrica*, vol. 85, 1996, p. 1076.

Shattock, Paul, and Gillian Lowdon. "Proteins, peptides, and autism: Part 2," *Brain Dysfunction*, no. 4, 1991, pp. 323-34. [Reviewed in *Autism Research Review International*, vol. 7, no. 1, 1993, pp. 4, 7.]

Shattock, Paul, et al. "Role of Neuropeptides in Autism and Their Relationships with Classical Neurotransmitters." *Brain Dysfunction,* vol. 3, 1990, p. 328.

Williams, Katherine, Paul Shattock, and Thomas Berney. "Proteins, peptides, and autism: Part 1." *Brain Dysfunction*, no. 4, 1991, pp. 320-22. [Reviewed in *Autism Research Review International*, vol. 7, no. 1, 1993, pp. 4,7.]

Anti-Yeast Therapy

The possible link between *Candida albicans* and autism, as well as other learning disabilities, is a topic of debate in the medical community. Some doctors call the "yeast syndrome" a fad, while other doctors claim to have helped many children by reducing an overabundance of yeast or related organisms in their systems.

Candida is a yeast-like fungus that is normally present in the body to some degree. Certain circumstances, however, may lead to an overgrowth of yeast that a normal, healthy immune system would otherwise suppress. Common symptoms of such an overgrowth are vaginal yeast infections and thrush (white patches sometimes present in the mouth of an infant). More severe symptoms of yeast overgrowth may include long-term immune system disturbances, depression, schizophrenia, and possibly autism.

Medical Complaints Associated with the Candida Complex

• Intestinal problems (constipation, diarrhea, flatulence)

• Distended stomach

• Excessive genital touching in infants and young children

• Cravings for carbohydrates, fruits and sweets. After ingestion of carbohydrates, hyperactivity for 15-20 minutes followed by hypoactivity

• Unpleasant odor of hair and feet, acetone smell from the mouth

• Skin rashes

• Fatigue, lethargy, depression, anxiety

• Insomnia

• Behavior problems

• May act "drunk"

• Hyperactivity [From Rimland/Mayo Letter.]

Candida overgrowth is often attributed to long-term antibiotic or hormonal treatments. It has been reported that some children whose autistic tendencies surfaced at 18-24 months had been continually treated with antibiotics to control chronic ear infections. Other possible causes of candida overgrowth: immunosuppressant drug therapy, exposure to herpes or chicken pox, exposure to toxins that might disrupt the immune system.

It may be hard to find a physician who is knowledgeable or accepting of the possible link between candida and severe learning and developmental disorders such as autism. However, Dr. Bernard Rimland of the Autism Research Institute has suggested that perhaps 5-10 % of children with autism whose medical profiles indicate the possibility of yeast overgrowth may see some improvement if properly treated for candida.

Doctors can recommend a stool analysis that tests for possible yeast overgrowth. Unfortunately, stool cultures are not always reliable. Doctors familiar with the treatment of yeast overgrowth will sometimes suggest a therapeutic trial of an antifungal medication. In this case, treatment is based on medical history or current symptoms that may indicate a yeast overgrowth. The patient is carefully monitored to see if the medication is useful.

Treatment for candida overgrowth usually includes prescription of an antifungal medication. Nystatin is commonly prescribed, but others are also available. In addition, certain herbal formulas are showing promising results in the control of yeast overgrowth. Yeast has been proven to be sensitive to gentian formulas, garlic, caprylic acid, undecenoic acid, and rutin. (These treatments are still considered "experimental.") Along with antifungal medications, a diet which eliminates sugar, yeast, and many other foods is a critical part of the treatment. Symptoms may grow worse at the onset of treatment but may gradually improve if candida overgrowth is in fact contributing to the patient's problems.

Finally, it is important to note that *Candida albicans* is not the only yeast that may cause problems. Stool analysis may reveal various species of yeast. A yeast overgrowth of any kind may cause serious problems in various functions of the body. For example, minerals such as copper may not be properly absorbed. Also, since yeast overgrowths can interfere with the body's ability to regulate the absorption of essential fatty acids, it may be prudent to request an analysis of short- and long-chain fatty acid absorption when testing for yeast overgrowth by means of stool culture. An excellent source of information on the autism/yeast connection is William Shaw's book, *Biological Treatments for Autism and PDD*. (See Resources, Great Plains Laboratory.)

RESOURCES

American Academy of Environmental Medicine (AAEM)
Kellog, Suite 625
Wichita, KS 67207
(316) 684-5500/(316) 684-5709 FAX
http://www.aaem.com
May be able to refer you to a physician knowledgeable about candida overgrowth. Send self-addressed stamped envelope with request.

American Association of Naturopathic Physicians
3201 New Mexico Av NW, Suite 350
Washington, DC 20016
(866) 538-2267/(202) 274-1992 FAX
http://www.naturopathic.org/
Can provide a list of naturopathic physicians or a referral to a registered physician in your area.

Autism Research Institute
4182 Adams Av
San Diego, CA 92116
(619) 281-7165
http://www.autism.com/ari
Can provide information on candida and autism. Packet includes candida questionnaire, newspaper articles on candida

and autism, dietary guidelines, and an editorial by Bernard Rimland on the subject.

Great Plains Laboratory
11813 West 77th
Lenexa, KS 66214
(913) 341-8949/(913) 341-6207 FAX
http://www.autism.com/shaw-yeast/
Dr. William Shaw, Director. Offers urine testing and treatment services for yeast overgrowth.

Great Smokies Diagnostic Laboratory
63 Zillicoa St
Asheville, NC 28801
(828) 253-0621
http://www.gsdl.com/
Can provide kit for stool analysis used for determining yeast overgrowth. Provides a very comprehensive profile of fatty acid absorption, and will also culture possible bacterial overgrowth. Can conduct sensitivity tests for the effects of antifungal drugs and "experimental" herbs on individual cultures.

Immuno Laboratories
1620 W Oakland Park Blvd
Ft. Lauderdale, FL 33311
(800) 476-4425
http://www.immunolabs.com
Dr. John Rebello, Director. A state, federal, and Medicare-licensed laboratory Immuno offers comprehensive diagnostic programs in the fields of allergy, immunology, and nutrition. Tests include IgG, IgE (food allergy blood tests) as well as Candida Albicans Assay.

SUGGESTED READING

Connolly, Pat. *The Candida Albicans Yeast-Free Cookbook*. New Canaan, CN: Keats Publishing, 1985.

Crook, William G. *Solving the Puzzle of Your Hard-To Raise Child*. New York: Random House, 1987.

———. *The Yeast Connection*. PO Box 3494, 681 Skyline Dr, Jackson, TN 38301: Professional Books, 1987.

Lewis, Lisa. *Special Diets for Special Kids*. Arlington, TX: Future Horizons, 1998. (800)489-0727.

Lorenzani, Shirley. *Candida: A Twentieth Century Disease*. New Canaan, CN: Keats Publishing, 1986.

Shaw, William. *Biological Treatments for Autism and PDD*. Overland Park, Kansas. Self-Published, 1998.

Rimland, Bernard. "Letter from the Autism Research Institute, Candida Packet" (original letter from Gus and Giana Mayo). San Diego: Autism Research Institute.

Shaw, William. *Biological Treatments for Autism and PDD*. Overland Park, Kansas. Self-Published, 1998.

Trowbridge, John P., and Walker Morton. *The Yeast Syndrome*. New York: Bantam Books, 1986.

Sensory/Physical Therapies

We interpret and integrate the world around us through our senses. However, children with autism suffer from severe sensory problems. They may hear sounds much more acutely than the normal person, hate the taste or texture of all but a few foods, or be intolerant of a simple hug. Discussed in this chapter are several therapeutic approaches that address the issue of sensory dysfunction.

Sensory Integration

Dr. Jean Ayers pioneered the theory that some children suffer from a neural disorder that causes the nervous system to receive incoming information, via the senses, in an inefficient manner. This disturbance, called Sensory Integrative Disorder (SID), is found in some individuals with autism.

Besides the obvious senses of sight, taste, touch, smell, and hearing, our nervous system also senses pressure, movement, body position, and the force of gravity. These senses are known as tactile (touch), vestibular (movement), and proprioceptive (body position). The tactile, vestibular, and proprioceptive systems work closely with other systems in our body and help us make appropriate responses to incoming sensations and to our environment. Sensory integration (SI) is the term used to define this complex process.

When sensory integration does not develop normally in a child, a number of difficulties may arise. Indicators of sensory integrative dysfunction may include:

• oversensitivity to touch, movements, sights, or sounds

• underreaction to sensory stimulation

• unusually high or low levels of activity

• coordination problems

• delays in speech, language, and motor skills

• behavior problems

• poor self concept

If sensory integrative problems are suspected, a child can be evaluated by a physical or occupational therapist who has received certification in SI therapy. For a list of qualified professionals, contact Sensory Integration International (address listed below). Many insurance policies will partially cover physical or occupational therapy. Also, there may be a therapist employed by your school district who has received SI certification. Even if your child is not attending school, he or she may qualify for their services.

Sensory integrative therapy (SIT) is highly individualized, with activities designed to meet the child's unique developmental needs. A very important component of SIT is that the therapist pays close attention to what motivates the child. Most children will be drawn to the activities that benefit them the most. If the child has difficulty choosing activities, the therapist provides more structure. Because SIT resembles play, most children enjoy it. Equipment may include swings, bolsters, slides, and scooterboards, and materials for fine motor activities are also available.

Successful therapy will increase the child's ability to integrate sensory information more efficiently. Improvements in motor coordination, language development, reduction of "hyper" or "hypo" responsiveness to sensory stimuli, better emotional adjustment, and self-confidence are possible benefits. Careful monitoring and documentation of your child's development should be conducted by the therapist. Treatment may last from six months to two years, depending on the unique needs of the child.

RESOURCES

The American Occupational Therapy Association (AOTA)
4720 Montgomery Ln
PO Box 31220
Bethesda, MD 20824-1220
(301) 652-2682
http://www.aota.org/
National organization of occupational therapists. Can provide listings of therapists in your region.

Center for Neurodevelopmental Studies
5430 West Glenn Dr
Glendale, AZ 85301
(602) 915-0345
http://www.cirs.org/homepage/cns/
Lorna Jean King, Director. Information available on sensory integrative therapy.

Developmental Concepts
PO Box 31759
Phoenix, AZ 85046-1759
(888) 287-3239/(602) 482-9851 FAX
http:// www.atready.com
Bonnie Hanschu, Director. Hanschu is the creator of the Ready Approach. Offers seminars, publications, products, and a newsletter related to sensory processing disorders. Offers a two-day course which compares autism and attention deficit disorder from a sensory perspective.

North American Riding for the Handicapped Association (Therapeutic Horseback Riding)
PO Box 33150
Denver, CO 80233
(800) 369-7433/(303) 252-4610 FAX
http://www.narha.org/
An association of accredited therapeutic horseback instructors who work with occupational therapists to provide sensory therapy through horseback riding for individuals with disabilities.

Sensory Integration International (SII)
PO Box 5339
Torrance, CA 90510-5339
(310) 787-8805/(310) 787-8130 FAX
http://home.earthlink.net/~sensoryint/
A nonprofit organization that provides general informa-

tion on sensory integration and information on specific subjects. Can also provide a list of occupational and physical therapists who have been certified in sensory integrative therapy. Publishes *Sensory Integration Quarterly*.

Sensory Resources
2200 E Patrick Lane, Suite 3A
Las Vegas, NV 89119
(888) 357-5867/(702) 891-8899 FAX
http://www.sensoryresources.com
A website dedicated to resources for raising children with sensory motor, developmental, and social-emotional challenges.

SUGGESTED READING

Anderson, Elizabeth, and Pauline Emmons. *Unlocking the Mysteries of Sensory Dysfunction: A Resource for Anyone Who Works with, or Lives with, a Child with Sensory Issues*. Arlington, TX: Future Horizons, 1996.

Ayres, A. Jean. *Sensory Integration and the Child*. Los Angeles: Western Psychological Services, 1983.

King, L.J. "Sensory integration: An effective approach to therapy and education." Autism Research Review International, vol. 5, no. 2, 1991, pp. 3, 6.

Kranowitz, Carol Stock. *The Out-of-Sync Child: Recognizing and Coping with Sensory Integration Dysfunction*. New York: Perigee, 1998.

Video

Reisman, Judith and Lorna Jean King. *Making Contact: Sensory Integration and Autism*. Available from Media Learning Systems, Continuing Education Programs of America, PO Box 52, Peoria, IL 61650, (309)263-0310.

Auditory Integration Training

Pioneered in France in the 1960's by Dr. Guy Berard, Auditory Integration Training (AIT) was introduced to the United States in 1990. AIT was brought to the attention of the general public in 1991, when Annabel Stehli's book, *The Sound of a Miracle: A Child's Triumph over Autism*, was published. Stehli's daughter, Georgie, who had been diagnosed with autism, eventually made dramatic improvements after receiving AIT.

AIT is currently available throughout the world, and there is growing evidence that many, but not all, children and adults with autism will benefit from this training. Drs. Bernard Rimland and Stephen M. Edelson have published three studies on the efficacy of AIT. A recent study supports earlier research showing AIT to be effective in reducing behavior problems and improving the brain's ability to process auditory information. [See Edelson, 2000.]

Other benefits from AIT reported by parents of children with autism include increased eye contact, spontaneous speech, socialization, and attention span, and a lessened sensitivity to certain sounds.

AIT includes a total of 10 hours of listening to modulated music over a 10-20 day period. Before receiving AIT the individual is given an audiogram, a test for hearing at various sound frequencies. According to Dr. Berard, a person may hear certain sound frequencies too well, and this may cause processing problems. In an audiogram, the frequencies that a person hears too well are referred to as "auditory peaks."

After the initial audiogram, the individual listens to music through a special machine by means of earphones. After five hours of listening, the individual is given another audiotest to see if auditory peaks are still present or if new ones have developed. Finally, a third audiotest is given at the end of the listening session to determine whether the individual's hearing has been normalized. [See Edelson, 1999.] If the individual with autism cannot complete the audiotest, a standard procedure available for setting the AIT machine without it. There are many different AIT machines. All of the machines vary the music's sound and frequencies. Some AIT machines also vary the volume level.

Experts are still not certain how or why AIT seems to reduce hearing hypersensitivity in some people. Theories suggest that AIT may train the person to shift his/her attention more efficiently, provide stimulation to specific auditory or vestibular centers in the brain, and/or enable the individual to adapt to loud sounds. Edelson and his colleagues have noted that AIT may be beneficial for individuals who are not sound sensitive as well as for those who are sensitive.

Not all persons will benefit from AIT. However, many families continue to note improvements in their children after they have received the training. The improvement is usually subtle and may take several months to be noticed. Some individuals, after receiving AIT, may exhibit behavior problems that may last anywhere from two days to two months. Dr. Edelson encourages parents to employ consistent behavior management strategies during this adjustment period. Often, positive gains in social, emotional, and academic development coincide with the difficult adjustment period. Continuing research will increase our understanding of this intervention.

RESOURCES

Autism Research Institute
4182 Adams Av
San Diego, CA 92116
(619)281-7165
http://www.autism.com/ari
Dr. Bernard Rimland, Director. Can provide a list of practitioners using the Berard AIT method. Will also send an information packet on Auditory Integration Training for $5.

Society for Auditory Intervention Techniques (SAIT)
PO Box 4538
Salem, OR 97302
http://www.sait.org
Dr. Stephen M. Edelson, President. The Society for Auditory Integration Techniques is dedicated to establishing guidelines and procedures. Provides parents and AIT practitioners with the latest information about various auditory interventions. Also distributes a quarterly newsletter. Membership is open to parents and professionals.

SUGGESTED READING

Berard, Guy. *Hearing Equals Behavior.* New Canaan, CT: Keats Publishing, 1982.

Edelson, Stephen M. "Auditory Integration Training: Basic Information & Additional Information." [The Center for the Study of Autism Website Publication, 2000. http://www.autism.com/csa]

Edelson, Stephen M., Deborah Arin, Margaret Bauman, Scott E. Lukas, Jane H. Rudy, Michelle Sholar, and Bernard Rimland. "Auditory Integration Training: A double-blind study of behavioral and electrophysiological effects in people with autism." *Focus on Autism and Other Developmental Disabilities*, vol. 14, No. 2, 1999 pp. 73-81.

Rimland, B., and S.M. Edelson. "Auditory Integration Training: A Pilot Study." *Journal of Autism and Developmental Disorders*, vol. 25, 1995, pp. 61-70.

———."The Effects of Auditory Integration Training in Autism." *American Journal of Speech-Language Pathology*, vol. 5, 1994, pp. 16-24.

Stehli, Annabel. *The Sound of a Miracle: A Child's Triumph over Autism.* New York: Doubleday, 1991.

Visual Interventions

Vision Therapy and Prism Lenses

There is an increasing awareness of the importance of vision exams for children with disabilities. Vision is more than being able to see things clearly. It involves eye coordination, perception and processing, focusing, tracking, and more. It is important for the child to be examined by a developmental optometrist who can check for developmental problems related to vision, not just for acuity.

Symptoms of visual difficulties may include:

• Eyes that cross or turn

• Covering or closing an eye in order to use only one, tilting or turning the head

• Looking at things out of the corners or sides of the eyes

• Blinking, grimacing, squinting, and other compensating behaviors

•Visual stimulation behaviors: finger flicking; obsession with spinning, patterns, or other visual effects

• Short attention span, avoidance of close work or other activities

• Low frustration level.

• Headaches, dizziness, nausea, car sickness and light sensitivity [See Brockett, "Vision Therapy . . ."]

There is no standard way to do vision training. The most popular method involves using yoked prism lenses while performing visual motor exercises. Yoked prism lenses displace the person's vision either up, down, left, or right by two to five degrees. Different from standard prescription lenses used for object identification, yoked prism lenses affect peripheral vision and depth perception, movement in space, and night vision. Yoked prism lenses can help an individual achieve better visual processing, thus leading to improvement in visual attention, depth perception, coordination, and overall body posture, among other things.

Vision training is also an effective method of treating strabismus (crossed eyes, one or both eyes turn inward or outward) which people with autism often exhibit. Strabismus cannot always be detected simply by looking at a person, but may need to be uncovered through testing from a qualified optometrist. Characteristics shared by people who may benefit from visual training include, but are not limited to: trouble walking up and down stairs, difficulty catching a ball, toe walking, looking at objects from the corner of the eye, and poor motor coordination.

Training usually consists of visual motor exercises that restructure the brain's interpretations of visual fields. The therapy itself usually consists of daily home exercise sessions and periodic checkups. Duration of treatment varies according to the needs of the individual. The first step is to obtain a vision evaluation by a behavioral or developmental optometrist. For a referral, contact the Developmental Delay Registry. [See Resources.]

Irlen Lenses

Educator Helen Irlen developed the concept of Scotopic Sensitivity Syndrome (SSS), which is a visual perception problem. Perceptual problems may stem from color (especially bright colors), the light source (e.g. fluorescent lights), luminance (e.g. reflection), contrast (e.g., black type on white paper), and intensity (brightness).

While Irlen was experimenting with ways to help adults overcome chronic learning disabilities, she discovered that covering their reading material with a transparent colored acetate sheet resulted in marked improvement in their reading abilities. Irlen refined this discovery into colored lenses, known as Irlen Lenses. The tinted lenses serve to filter out certain light frequencies, which enhances the wearer's visual perception, and thus increases general comfort level. While some developmental or behavioral optometrists occasionally prescribe tinted lenses to decrease light sensitivity, Irlen has developed an elaborate assessment procedure to determine the appropriate tint for each person. At Irlen Clinics, the individual is screened for symptoms of Scotopic Sensitivity Syndrome. Irlen lists some of the symptoms of SSS as:

• light sensitivity

• poor depth perception

• contrast and color sensitivity

• restricted span of recognition

• inefficient reading

• distortions (images moving, changing, jumping, disappearing, or sparkling)

If it is determined that SSS is present, the clinicians determine the proper tint for the filtered lenses. There are hundreds of different possibilities and each individual's needs are unique. Although there is lack of research data on use the Irlen Lenses for people with autism, many adults with autism report improvement and relief from visual processing problems.

RESOURCES

Center for Visual Management
Dr. Melvin Kaplan, OD
150 White Plains Rd

Tarrytown, NY 10591
(914)631-1070
http://www.autisticvision.com/index.htm
Dr. Kaplan specializes in developmental vision problems, and is one of the leading authorities in this field.

Developmental Delay Registry

4401 Eastwest Hwy, Suite 207
Bethesda, MD 20814
(301)652-2263/(301)652-9133 FAX
http://www.devdelay.org
Provides a referral list of qualified behavioral or developmental optometrists.

Parents Active for Vision Education (PAVE)

4135 54th Pl
San Diego, CA 92105-2303
(800)PAVE-988/ (619)287-0084 FAX
http://www.pave-eye.com/vision/
A nonprofit resource and support organization whose mission is to raise public awareness of learning-related vision problems and the crucial relationship between vision and achievement. Free pamphlet. Video, "Vision Alert: 20/20 is not Enough!" Available for $35.

Irlen Institute

5380 Village Rd
Long Beach, CA 90808
(562)496-2550/(562)429-8699 FAX
http://www.irlen.com
Helen Irlen, Director. Works extensively with individuals with autism. Affiliated clinics worldwide.

SUGGESTED READING

Brockett, Sally. "Vision Therapy: A Beneficial Intervention for Developmental Disabilities." [The Center for the Study of Autism Website Publication http://www.autism.com/csa]

Edelson, Stephen. "Interview with Melvin Kaplan, O.D." [Center for the Study of Autism Publication, 1996. http://www.autism.com/csa]

Irlen, Helen. *Reading by the Colors*. Garden City Park, NY: Avery Publishing Group, 1991.

Kaplan, M., B., Rimland, and S.M. Edelson. "Strabismus in autism." *Focus on Autism and Other Developmental Disabilities,* vol. 14, 1999, pp. 124-40.

Kaplan, M., S.M. Edelson, J. Lydia Seip. "Behavioral changes in autistic individuals as a result of wearing ambient transitional prism lenses." *Child Psychiatry and Human Development*, vol. 29, Fall 1998, pp. 65-76.

Kaplan, Melvin. "Visual model for children with neurointegrative dysfunction," *The Advocate,* vol. 27, no. 1, 1995, pp. 25-26.

Rose, Marcy, and Nancy G. Torgerson, "A behavioral approach to vision and autism." *Journal of Optometric Vision Development,* vol. 25, no. 4, 1994, pp. 269-75.

Schulman, Randy L., "Optometry's role in the treatment of autism," *Journal of Optometric Vision Development,* vol. 25, no. 4, 1994, pp. 259-68.

Osteopathy/Craniosacral SM Therapy

In the early 1970s, Dr. John E. Upledger, an osteopathic physician and surgeon, developed a light-touch, manipulative therapy, which he termed "craniosacral therapy." Osteopathy is a similar therapy in which gentle manipulation is given to various parts of the body to free restrictions of motion.

Some of Upledger's techniques are based on the work of Dr. William Sutherland. His work, known as "cranial osteopathy," involves manipulation of the bones of the cranium. Sutherland believed that the bones in the skull evolved to provide opportunity for their movement and that, when their movement becomes restricted for various reasons, head pains, coordination difficulties, and other problems may occur.

In 1975, Upledger and other scientists at Michigan State University's College of Osteopathic Medicine investigated Sutherland's theory that skull bones move in response to the hydraulic pressure of the cerebrospinal fluid. The team concluded that the skull's sutures are not hardened structures, but are indeed elastic, containing nerve fibers, blood vessels, and elastic tissue.

Upledger expanded his work on the bones of the skull, face, and mouth (cranium) to include the bones in the spinal cord and down to the sacrum and coccyx, all of which he includes in the craniosacral system. He also views the brain and spinal cord as connected by a hydraulic system encased in three tough membranes, which are separated from one another by fluid-filled spaces. According to Upledger, movement of the fluid up and down the spinal cord creates movement in the membranes which, in turn, affects the body's connective tissue. An imbalance in the craniosacral system can affect the development of the brain and spinal cord, which, in turn, can result in various bodily dysfunctions. Craniosacral therapy provides a way to examine movements in the various parts of the system and to free them from restrictions by means of gentle pressure from the therapist.

Upledger has conducted studies on children with autism to determine if there is any correlation between such restrictions and the presence autism in this population. He believes that children who are considered "classically autistic" in behavioral terms show similar patterns of restriction in the craniosacral system. [See Upledger and Vredevoogd, pp. 262-64.] According to Upledger and in anecdotal reports from parents, improvements in behaviors such as head-banging and wrist-biting have been noted in children after they received craniosacral therapy. Also reported are improvements in communication and lessening of hyperactivity. With more research in this field, the effectiveness of this treatment for autism may be further substantiated. In looking into osteopathy or cranialsacral therapy, it is important to seek out only well-trained and certified practitioners.

RESOURCES

American Osteopathic Association
142 East Ontario Street, Chicago, IL 60611
(800)621-1773/(312)202-8200 FAX
http://www.aoa-net.org/index.htm
Provides information and referrals on osteopathy.

Craniosacral Therapy Association, United Kingdom
Monomark House,
27 Old Gloucester Street,
LONDON, WC1N 3XX.

Tel. 07000 784 735
http://www.craniosacral.co.uk/
Provide support for practitioners of craniosacral therapy.
Can provide referrals.

Osteopathic Centre for Children
109 Harley Street
London, UK W1G 6AN
Tel. 0207 486 6160
http://www.occ.uk.com
A Registered Charity whose clinic staff treat children with
many disabilities, including autism. Treatment is based
on the work of William Sutherland and others.

The Upledger Institute
11211 Prosperity Farm Rd, Suite 325
Palm Beach Gardens, FL 33410-3487
(800)233-5880/561-622-4771 FAX
http://upledger.com/
Works with individuals and offers information on the
work of Dr. Upledger. Also trains practitioners in the use
of craniosacral therapy. Can refer you to a practitioner in
your area.

SUGGESTED READING

Reuben, Carolyn. "Craniosacral therapy: Adjusting the
bones in the skull can affect the way you feel and act."
East/West, Oct. 1987, pp. 22-25.

The Upledger Institute. "Discover the CranioSacral System." Palm Beach Gardens, FL, 1988.

Upledger, John E. "Craniosacral function in brain dysfunction." *Osteopathic Annals*, vol. 11, no. 7, 1983, pp. 318-24.

Upledger, John E., and Jon D. Vredevoogd. *Craniosacral Therapy*. Seattle: Eastland Press, 1983.

Intensive Interventions

The methods listed in this chapter are only four of the many intensive approaches that may be beneficial for children with autism. At this time, scientific research on their efficacy for improving autism is scant, yet they have endured with varying degrees of popularity as possible interventions. As with any intervention, a parent should carefully consider all aspects of a therapeutic approach before choosing it as a means to help their child.

Greenspan Method

Dr. Stanley Greenspan, a child psychiatrist has developed a relationship-based, interactive form of therapy that is highly individualized. Greenspan's D.I.R. (Developmental, Individual-Difference, Relationship-Based model) has the goal of helping children form a sense of themselves as "intentional, interactive individuals and develop cognitive language and social capabilities from this basic sense of intentionality." [See Greenspan, 1985.] On the basis of a model of functional development,

Greenspan specifies certain milestones of development in this order:

- self-regulation and interest in the world

- intimacy

- two-way communication

- complex communication

- emotional ideas

- emotional thinking

What Greenspan calls "floor-time" is a one-on-one experience between the child and a parent or therapist, usually lasting between 20-30 minutes. During floor-time, the adult focuses on relationship-based interaction, often following the child's lead or interest in order to engage in play that encourages communication, logical thought, attention, and the expression of feelings and ideas. Although there is a lack of controlled studies at this time, in his book book, *The Child with Special Needs*, Greenspan reports on the success rates of children who participated in his program for two or more years.

RESOURCES

Dr. Stanley Greenspan
4938 Hampden Ln, Box 229
Bethesda, MD 20814
(301)320-6360
http://www.stanleygreenspan.com
Information available on the Greenspan method.

SUGESTED READING

Greenspan, Stanley, Serena Wieder, and Robin Simmons. *The Child with Special Needs: Encouraging Intellectual and Emotional Growth.* Reading, MA: Addison Wesley, 1998.

Greenspan, Stanley. "A Developmental Approach to Problems in Relating and Communicating in Autistic Spectrum Disorders and Related Syndromes." *Spotlight on Topics in Developmental Disabilities,* vol. 1, no. 4, 1985, p. 5.

The Son-Rise Program®

Barry Neil Kaufman and Samahria Kaufman, founders of The Option Institute and Fellowship, pioneered their own method of working with children with autism in the early 1970s, when they helped their son, Raun, overcome autism using an intensive, one-on-one approach. In his book, *Son-Rise: The Miracle Continues*, Barry Neil Kaufman, recounts not only their story, but the stories of others who have used the Son-Rise Program.

The Son-Rise Program, based on a loving, non-judgmental attitude, encourages following the child's lead or actions while simultaneously motivating him or her to expand his/her world. High-energy play sessions in an environment geared specifically for a child with autism, on a full-day intensive basis, are features of a home-based Son-Rise Program. The central idea is that the child will be motivated to find ways to reach out to parents and volunteers trained to present a consistent attitude of acceptance and enthusiasm.

The Option Institute and Fellowship offers training

for families wishing to create home-based Son-Rise Programs. The Son-Rise Programs are *highly individualized*. Parents observe staff members interacting with their children, and practice sessions for parents are also built into the program.

Learning the Optiva Dialogue[SM] process is another component. In this process, parents are encouraged to explore their situation and question limiting judgments or beliefs they may hold about themselves and/or their situation. At present, no formal studies or evaluations have validated the effectiveness of the Son-Rise Program as a treatment for children with autism.

RESOURCES

The Option Institute and Fellowship
2080 S Undermountain Rd
Sheffield, MA 01257
(413)229-2100/(413)229-8931 FAX
http://www.option.org
The Option Institute offers many books and tapes that explain the Kaufmans' philosophy and methods of working with special children, as well as other books about the Option Process®.

SUGGESTED READING

Kaufman, Barry Neil. *Son-Rise: The Miracle Continues*. Tiburon, CA: H.J. Kramer, 1994.

———. *To Love is To Be Happy With*. New York: Ballantine Books, 1977.

———. *Happiness Is A Choice*. New York: Ballantine Books, Random House, 1991.

The Option Institute and Fellowship. "The Son-Rise Program®," Sheffield, MA, 1993.

Daily Life Therapy

Developed by the late Dr. Kiyo Kitahara of Japan, Daily Life Therapy is a method that provides children with a structured educational model through group dynamics, modeling, and physical activity. Currently, the Boston Higashi School and the Musashino Higashi School in Japan utilize Daily Life Therapy in their day schools and residential programs.

The major components of Daily Life Therapy include:

• Vigorous physical exercise to reduce anxiety, gain stamina, and establish rhythm and routines

• Delivering sensory integration and vestibular stimulation services with emphasis on body position and movement, posture and equilibrium, perception and motor planning

• Group education with an emphasis on individuality and self-reliance, learning through imitation and the use of role models

• Instruction in language arts, math, social studies, science, and computer skills

• Vocational training

RESOURCES

Boston Higashi School
800 N Main St
(781)961-0800/(781) 961-0888
Randolph, MA 02368
http://www.bostonhigashi.org
Robert A. Fantasia, Director. Call or contact for information on Daily Life Therapy.

Honormead Schools Ltd.
The Grange, Hospital Ln
Mickleover, Derby, DE3 5DR
United Kingdom
01332 510951/01332 512867
School in the UK using Daily Life Therapy.

Musashino Higashi Gakuen School
3-25-3 Nishikubo
Musashino City, Tokyo 180
Japan
0422-54-8611/0422-51-0267 FAX
School in Japan using Daily Life Therapy.

SUGGESTED READING

Edwards, D. "The efficacy of Daily Life Therapy at the Boston Higashi School." *Therapeutic Approaches to Autism: Research and Practice. Collected Conference Papers*. Sunderland, UK: Autism Research Unit, 1995, pp. 115-27.

Kitahara, K. *Daily Life Therapy: A Method of Educating Autistic Children, Volumes I-III*. Boston, MA: Nimrod Press, 1984.

Roland, C.C., G.G. McGee, T.R. Risley, and B. Rimland. "Description of the Tokyo Higashi Program for Autistic Children." Autism Research Institute Publication, San Diego: CA, 1987.

The Doman/Delacato Method

The Institute for the Achievement of Human Potential, in Philadelphia, was founded in the early 1960s by Glenn Doman, Robert Doman, and Carl Delacato. The team concluded that there were many forms of brain injury, the form depending on the area of the brain affected and the extent of the damage. Departing from the theories of that time, which approached brain injury from an all-or-nothing standpoint and considered it incurable, the Institute identified children according to the severity of their brain dysfunction:

• **Mild.** Suffering from perceptual problems (how the world is perceived via the senses)

• **Moderate.** Able to move and make sounds; detectable by medical testing

• **Severe.** Unable to move or make sounds, obvious lack of bodily functions [Delacato, *The Ultimate Stranger.*]

The Doman/Delacato theory holds that the brain can develop only if it is used. In order to develop properly, it must receive the necessary stimulation. To treat children or adults brought to them for help, they devised ways to let them reexperience normal stages of development by stimulating the brain through movement of the body. For instance, if children could not walk well, they gave them the opportunity to learn to crawl. The widely known term, "patterning," refers to the manipulation of someone's body in imitation of creeping or crawling movements when the person is unable to make these movements on their own.

Patterning used to mean 14-hour marathons of volunteers working with a child or adult. Unless there is a truly severe injury, new techniques often require less time, usually an hour or two of organized programming per day. Most of the treatment was then, and is today, carried out in home programs by the parents.

It is important to note that the Doman/Delacato Method has come under intense, critical scrutiny. Despite the fact that this method has been in existence for over thirty years, controlled research is lacking.

RESOURCES

Delacato International
Consultants in Learning
306 Williams Rd
Fort Washington, PA 19034
(215)540-9252/(215)540-9253 FAX
http://www.delacato.net
Carl Delacato and Robert Delacato, Directors. Can provide information on international centers. Works with children with brain injuries and autism.

The Institute For the Achievement of Human Potential
8801 Stenton Av
Wyndmoor, PA 19038
(215)233-2050
http://www.iahp.org/
Glenn Doman, Director. Works with individuals with brain injury. Can provide a list of affiliated institutes.

SUGGESTED READING

American Academy of Pediatrics, "The Doman-Delacato Treatment of Neurologically Handicapped Children (RE2709)," vol. 70, no. 5 November, 1982, pp. 810-12.

Delacato, Carl. *The Ultimate Stranger*. New York: Doubleday, 1974, 1984.

Doman, Glenn. *What to Do About Your Brain-Injured Child*. New York: Doubleday, 1974, 1990.

Melton, David. *Todd*. Englewood Cliffs, NJ: Prentice-Hall, 1968.

Music Interventions

Music Therapy

Individuals with autism have been treated with music therapy for many years now with varying degrees of success. Most popular in Europe, it is practiced worldwide. Music therapy seeks to use music as a facilitating agent, or therapeutic tool, to further growth and development in the client. Registered music therapists must undergo a college education, which includes courses in musicianship, behavioral and social sciences, as well as internship in a music therapy program. [See Boxhill, pp. 2-3.]

Music therapy in any individual case may include many activities, among them singing, movement to music, and playing instruments. Proponents of music therapy believe for a number of reasons that music can be used successfully as a medium for helping individuals with developmental disabilities, including autism. Among the reasons given are the following:

• **Music therapy requires no verbal interaction** although it may eventually facilitate it.

• **By nature, music is structured**, and it can facilitate structure in the environment in which it is experienced. Sound stimulus can aide in sensory integration because it involves all the senses. The vestibular system is also stimulated when rhythmic movement is included in the therapy.

• **Music naturally facilitates play** and therefore enhances learning through play.

• **Music therapy can aid in socialization and influence behavior.**

In general, music therapists hope to improve various aspects of a client's physical and mental health and to foster desired changes in behavior. A qualified music therapist makes a careful assessment of the individual's present capabilities and, on that basis, defines program goals, both long- and short-term. Music therapy can be carried out in a private setting, but it can also be incorporated into a child's program at school. [See Lathom.] An interested parent could also learn techniques for using music as a teaching tool at home. [See Meilahn, pp. 19-20.]

Rhythmic Entrainment Intervention

Developed by Jeff Strong, Rhythmic Entrainment Intervention (REI), is a musical therapy program which uses specific rhythmic patterns performed on a hand drum to aid individuals with neurobiological disorders, including autism and related developmental disabilities. REI combines ancient therapeutic drumming techniques and modern music and rhythm research.

The REI Institute offers two distinct tools: the REI Program and the Calming Rhythms audio recording. The REI Program is a custom-made recording of rhythms selected for each individual client. The Calming Rhythms audio recording, designed to alleviate anxiety and anxiety-based behaviors, is available as a prerecorded cassette or compact disc. Though at present there are no published scientific studies that support the effectiveness of this intervention, the REI website contains results from research studies conducted in various settings, including one at a Minnesota public school, where positive gains were noted. (See Resources.)

RESOURCES

American Music Therapy Association
8455 Colesville Rd, Suite 1000
Silver Spring, MD 20910
(301)589-3300/(301) 589-5175 FAX
http://www.musictherapy.org/
Founded in 1950. Aims to establish qualifications and standards of training for music therapists. Maintains placement services. Will send information on particular topics on request.

The Nordoff-Robbins Music Therapy Centre
2 Lissenden Gardens
London NW5 IPP
United Kingdom
071-267-4496
http://www.nordoff-robbins.org.uk/
Offers private and group music therapy classes for individuals with autism and other disabilities.

REI Institute
55 Lime Kiln Rd
Lamy, NM 87540
(800)659-6644
http://www.reiinstitute.com
Jeff Strong, President. Offers several program options, from custom-made recordings to generalized relaxation tapes, developed for individuals with neurological conditions such as autism, ADHD, and chronic pain.

SUGGESTED READING

Alvin, Julliette and Warwick, Auriel. *Music Therapy for the Autistic Child*. New York: Oxford University Press, 1991.

Boxhill, Edith Hillman. *Music Therapy for the Developmentally Disabled*. Rockville, MD: Aspen Publishers, 1985.

——. Music Therapy for Living: *The Principle of Normalization Embodied in Music Therapy*. St. Louis, MO: MMB Music, Inc., 1989.

Bruscia, Kenneth E. *Defining Music Therapy*. Phoenixville, PA: Barcelona Publishers, 1989.

Croall, Jonathan. "The Sound of Silence," *The London Times Educational Supplement*, Sept. 20, 1991.

Davis, William B., Gfeller, Kate and Thaut, Michail H. *An Introduction to Music Therapy: Theory and Practice*. Dubuque, IA: William C. Brown Publishers, 1992.

Lathom, Wanda. *The Role of Music Therapy in the Education of Handicapped Children and Youth*, Report of

The National Association for Music Therapy. Lawrence, KS, 1980.

Meilahn, Daniel C. "Music and the autistic child: A family affair," *The Advocate*, vol. 18, no. 5, 1986, pp.19-20.

Nordoff, Paul, and Clive Robbins. *Music Therapy in Special Education.* New York: John Day, 1971.

———. *Creative Music Therapy.* New York: John Day, 1976.

Peters, Jacqueline Schmidt. *Music Therapy: An Introduction.* Springfield, IL: Charles C. Thomas, 1987.

Schalkwijk, F.W. *Music and People with Developmental Disabilities: Music Therapy, Remedial Music Making and Musical Activities.* Bristol, PA: Jessica Kingsley Publishers, 1994.

Schulberg, Cecilia H. *The Music Therapy Sourcebook.* New York: Human Sciences Press, 1981.

Streeter, Elaine. Making Music with the Young Child with Special Needs. Bristol, PA: Jessica Kingsley Publishers, 1993.

Relaxation Techniques

All of us face stress and anxiety in our lives. However, some people with autism often suffer from severe stress and anxiety. This could be due to many factors, including problems with sensory processing, lack of understanding/confusion, or an inability to communicate effectively.

Professionals often emphasize that learning is optimal when one is calm and alert. In our changing world, full of visual, auditory, and other stimulation, relaxation techniques may indeed serve as important coping tools for all of us, and especially people with autism. Simple things, such as deep breathing, back rubs, foot massages, and warm baths can be integrated into one's daily routine and cost nothing.

Many people believe that various techniques such as massage, acupressure, or yoga, promote relaxation. The University of Miami School of Medicine's Touch Research Institute found that, compared to a control group, toddlers with autism showed improvements in socialization and imitation after a thirty-minute massage two times a week for five weeks. [See Field, et al.]

Biofeedback, a technique which seeks to increase an individual's self-awareness and in turn regulate bodily functions, has been used for many years to help individuals manage anxiety, depression, headaches, and muscle tension, among other ailments. Practitioners report that increased use of this technique helps individuals with attention and behavior problems, as well as learning disabilities, epilepsy and autism. [See Grierson & Othmer.]

The Work of June Groden

For over 20 years, June Groden has been a pioneer in the use of relaxation techniques for children and adults with autism and other developmental disorders. Drawing from the work of Edmond Jacobson, who developed the technique of Progressive Relaxation training in the 1930's, the relaxation program used at the Groden Center teaches individuals how to differentiate between tense muscles and relaxed muscles. Regularly scheduled one-on-one teaching sessions are employed. Depending on the attention span of the individual, the length of the sessions can last from a few minutes to twenty minutes. The individual is taught to tighten and relax the arms, hands, and legs and to do deep breathing in a sitting position.

After the individual has gained mastery of the relaxation procedure, a stress survey is administered to identify situations which might cause stress for a particular individual. Once identified, the person is taught coping strategies, such as relaxation or visual imagery to help reduce stress. The visual imagery component utilizes a procedure called picture rehearsal. The picture rehearsal might include a written script using line drawings or photographs to depict an event, the desired behavior, and finally the consequences. [See Edelson.]

Despite misconceptions that relaxation and visual imagery techniques might be of little benefit to people severely affected by autism, Groden has published many studies on its success. However, this is not an overnight process. Therapists at the Groden Center may work with clients over the course of many years. The Groden Center conducts workshops on relaxation techniques and offers training tools as well. (See Resources.)

The Work of Temple Grandin

Many individuals with autism show tactile defensiveness and a reluctance to be held. The hug machine (formerly named the squeeze machine) is a device used to give deep pressure stimulation, which may have a calming effect on some individuals with autism and increase their tolerance for human touch. The hug machine was invented by Dr. Temple Grandin, a woman with autism who is now a professor at Colorado State University. She is considered one of the foremost experts in the design and construction of livestock handling facilities.

In her books, *Thinking In Pictures* and *Emergence: Labeled Autistic*, Grandin describes her desire as a young child for deep pressure stimulation, but how she also felt overwhelmed by the sensory stimulation of an embrace. She writes that as a five year old she would dream of a machine that could apply the comforting pressure she longed for. In her teens, Grandin visited her aunt's ranch, where she noticed that cattle would sometimes relax when pressure was applied to them in a squeeze chute. She decided to try the cattle chute herself and found that it offered her relief from nervousness and anxiety. At age 18 she built a prototype hug machine and successfully used it to reduce her tactile defensiveness. After she gradually learned to tolerate being held by the machine, she was able to tolerate being touched or hugged by people.

Over the years Dr. Grandin perfected the hug machine. It is a fully padded, V-shaped device that is designed to apply pressure over most of the body. The user of the machine is in complete control and can adjust the amount of pressure the machine applies. Pressure is controlled by a lever-operated pneumatic valve, which is connected to an air cylinder that pulls the side boards together. The pressure remains constant, even when the user shifts position. [See Grandin, "Calming effects. . .," p. 65.]

It is interesting to note that Dr. Grandin began her design career with livestock handling equipment as the result of channeling her intense interest or "fixation" with cattle chutes and the hug machine. A caring, compassionate teacher encouraged her to learn all she could about why the machine had a calming effect. Because she was so interested in this, she eventually chose a career in animal science. Grandin believes that fixations can serve as motivators for learning. Instead of trying to stamp out a child's narrow interest, she encourages parents and teachers to broaden those interests into constructive activities. For instance, she suggests that if a child is interested in vacuum cleaners, an instructional manual for vacuums might make an engaging textbook for that child. Grandin writes that if she had not been encouraged to develop and understand her fixation with the hug machine she "might be sitting somewhere rotting in front of a TV instead of writing this chapter." [Grandin, in Schopler et al., p. 115.]

Although there is a limited number of formal research data on the effectiveness of the hug machine, some studies have concluded that the hug machine reduces hyperactivity and tactile defensiveness in some children with autism. [See Imamura et al.] Anecdotal reports suggest that the hug machine may be a beneficial component of sensory integrative therapy. Grandin states, ". . .the squeeze machine should be considered a novel treatment that has not been subjected to careful evaluation of clinical efficacy or safety." [Grandin, "Calming effects. . .," p. 70.] However, the machine is now commercially available.

RESOURCES

Biofeedback Certification Institute of America (BCIA)
10200 W 44th Ave, #310
Wheat Ridge, CO 80033-2840
(303)420-2902/(303)422-8894 FAX
http://www.bcia.org
Offers listing of certified biofeedback and neurofeedback practitioners nationwide.

Center for Neurodevelopmental Studies
5430 West Glenn Dr
Glendale, AZ 85301
(602)915-0345
http://www.cirs.org/homepage/cns/
Lorna Jean King, Founder. Can provide information on sensory integrative therapy. The center has used the hug machine in a sensory integrative program for children with autism and children with hyperactive behavior.

EEG Spectrum, Inc.
21601 Vanowen St, Suite 100
Canoga Park, CA 91303
(818)789-3456/(818) 728-0944 FAX
www.eegspectrum.com
Offers professional training, instrumentation, clinical services, and a referral network.

The Groden Center
86 Mount Hope Av
Providence, RI 02906
(401) 274-6310
http://www.grodencenter.org
June Groden, Director. Offers information and training on relaxation techniques for people with autism. Sells books and videos on this subject.

Therafin Corporation
19747 Wolf Rd
Mokena, IL 60448
(708)479-7300
http://www.therafin.com/
Manufactures and markets the hug machine. Write or call for information and price.

SUGGESTED READING

Books

Grandin, Temple. *Thinking in Pictures: And Other Reports from My Life with Autism.* New York: Doubleday, 1995.

Grandin, Temple, and Margaret Scariano. *Emergence: Labeled Autistic.* Arena Press, 20 Commercial Blvd, Novato, CA: 1986 (updated 1989).

Articles

Creedon, Margaret P. "Studies Related to Use of Lateral Pressure Equipment ('Hug Machine') By Day School Students with Autism," Program: Michael Reese Hospital and Medical Center, Developmental Institute, 1997. [From http://www.autism.com/csa]

Edelson, S.M., Edelson, M.G., Kerr, D., & Grandin, T., "Physiological and behavioral changes of deep pressure: A pilot study investigating the efficacy of Temple Grandin's Hug Machine." *American Journal of Occupational Therapy*, vol. 53, 1999, pp. 145-152.

Edelson, Stephen M. "An Interview with June Groden." The Center for the Study of Autism Publication. Salem: OR, 1997. [From the Center's website: http://www.autism.com/csa]

Field, T., et al. "Brief Report: Autistic Children's Attentiveness and Responsivity Improve after Touch Therapy," *Journal of Autism and Developmental Disorders*, vol. 27, 1997, pp. 333-38. [Cited in Waltz, Mitzi. *Pervasive Developmental Disorders*. O'Reilly, 1999.]

Grandin, Temple. "Calming effects of deep touch pressure in patients with autistic disorder, college students, and animals." *Journal of Child and Adolescent Psychopharmacology,* vol. 2, no. 1, 1992.

——. "An Inside View of Autism," in *High-Functioning Individuals with Autism.* Schopler, Eric, and Gary Mesibov [eds.]. New York: Plenum Press, 1992.

Grierson, Caroline, and Siegfried Othmer. "Biofeedback–The Ultimate Self-Help Discipline." EEG Spectrum, Inc. Publication, Encino, CA, 1999. [From www.eegspectrum.com]

Groden, J., and P. LeVasseur. "Cognitive picture rehearsal: A visual system to teach self-control." *In Teaching Children with Autism: Methods to Enhance Learning, Communication and Socialization.* K.A. Quill. [ed.]. Albany, NY: Delmar, 1995.

Imamura, K.N., T. Wiess, and D. Parham. "The effects of hug machine usage on behavioral organization of children with autism and autistic-like characteristics." *Sensory Integration Quarterly*, vol. 27, 1990, pp. 1-5.

Videos

Groden, J., J. Cautela, and G. Groden. "Breaking the barriers I: Relaxation techniques for people with special needs." Videotape. Champaign, IL: Research Press, 1989.

———. "Breaking the barriers, II: Imagery procedures for people with special needs." Videotape. Champaign, IL: Research Press, 1991.

Autism Treatment Evaluation Checklist (ATEC)
Bernard Rimland, Ph.D. and Stephen M. Edelson, Ph.D.

Autism Research Institute
4182 Adams Avenue, San Diego, CA 92116
fax: (619) 563-6840; www.autism.com/ari

Project/Purpose:				
Scores: I	II	III	IV	Total

This form is intended to measure the effects of treatment. Free scoring of this
form is available on the Internet at: www.autism.com/atec

Name of Child _____ _____ ☐ Male   Age _____
Last   First   ☐ Female   Date of Birth _____
Form completed by: _____ Relationship: _____ Today's Date _____

Please circle the letters to indicate how true each phrase is:

I. Speech/Language/Communication: [N] Not true   [S] Somewhat true   [V] Very true

N S V 1. Knows own name
N S V 2. Responds to 'No' or 'Stop'
N S V 3. Can follow some commands
N S V 4. Can use one word at a time (No!, Eat, Water, etc.)
N S V 5. Can use 2 words at a time (Don't want, Go home)
N S V 6. Can use 3 words at a time (Want more milk)
N S V 7. Knows 10 or more words
N S V 8. Can use sentences with 4 or more words
N S V 9. Explains what he/she wants
N S V 10. Asks meaningful questions
N S V 11. Speech tends to be meaningful/relevant
N S V 12. Often uses several successive sentences
N S V 13. Carries on fairly good conversation
N S V 14. Has normal ability to communicate for his/her age

II. Sociability: [N] Not descriptive   [S] Somewhat descriptive   [V] Very descriptive

N S V 1. Seems to be in a shell – you cannot reach him/her
N S V 2. Ignores other people
N S V 3. Pays little or no attention when addressed
N S V 4. Uncooperative and resistant
N S V 5. No eye contact
N S V 6. Prefers to be left alone
N S V 7. Shows no affection
N S V 8. Fails to greet parents
N S V 9. Avoids contact with others
N S V 10. Does not imitate
N S V 11. Dislikes being held/cuddled
N S V 12. Does not share or show
N S V 13. Does not wave 'bye bye'
N S V 14. Disagreeable/not compliant
N S V 15. Temper tantrums
N S V 16. Lacks friends/companions
N S V 17. Rarely smiles
N S V 18. Insensitive to other's feelings
N S V 19. Indifferent to being liked
N S V 20. Indifferent if parent(s) leave

III. Sensory/Cognitive Awareness: [N] Not descriptive   [S] Somewhat descriptive   [V] Very descriptive

N S V 1. Responds to own name
N S V 2. Responds to praise
N S V 3. Looks at people and animals
N S V 4. Looks at pictures (and T.V.)
N S V 5. Does drawing, coloring, art
N S V 6. Plays with toys appropriately
N S V 7. Appropriate facial expression
N S V 8. Understands stories on T.V.
N S V 9. Understands explanations
N S V 10. Aware of environment
N S V 11. Aware of danger
N S V 12. Shows imagination
N S V 13. Initiates activities
N S V 14. Dresses self
N S V 15. Curious, interested
N S V 16. Venturesome - explores
N S V 17. "Tuned in" — Not spacey
N S V 18. Looks where others are looking

IV. Health/Physical/Behavior: Use this code: [N] Not a Problem   [MI] Minor Problem   [MO] Moderate Problem   [S] Serious Problem

N MI MO S 1. Bed-wetting
N MI MO S 2. Wets pants/diapers
N MI MO S 3. Soils pants/diapers
N MI MO S 4. Diarrhea
N MI MO S 5. Constipation
N MI MO S 6. Sleep problems
N MI MO S 7. Eats too much/too little
N MI MO S 8. Extremely limited diet
N MI MO S 9. Hyperactive
N MI MO S 10. Lethargic
N MI MO S 11. Hits or injures self
N MI MO S 12. Hits or injures others
N MI MO S 13. Destructive
N MI MO S 14. Sound-sensitive
N MI MO S 15. Anxious/fearful
N MI MO S 16. Unhappy/crying
N MI MO S 17. Seizures
N MI MO S 18. Obsessive speech
N MI MO S 19. Rigid routines
N MI MO S 20. Shouts or screams
N MI MO S 21. Demands sameness
N MI MO S 22. Often agitated
N MI MO S 23. Not sensitive to pain
N MI MO S 24. "Hooked" or fixated on certain objects/topics
N MI MO S 25. Repetitive movements (stimming, rocking, etc.)

Appendix

National Organizations

The ARC
(Formerly the Association for Retarded Citizens)
1010 Wayne Ave, Suite 650
Silver Spring, MD 20910
(301)565-3842/(301)565-5342 FAX
 http://www.thearc.org/
Coordinates a network of local chapters. Provides information and advocacy. Local chapters may offer respite care programs and other opportunities for persons with severe disabilities.

Asperger Syndrome Coalition
PO Box 351268
Jacksonville, FL 32235-1668
(866)4-ASPRGR
http://www.asperger.org

The Association for Persons with Severe Handicaps (TASH)
29 W Susquehanna Av, Suite 210
Baltimore, MD 21204
(410)828-TASH/(410)828-6706 FAX
http://www.TASH.org/
An organization of parents and professionals working for the rights of all people with severe handicaps. Publishes a newsletter and a professional journal which include topics concerning autism.

Autism National Committee (AutCom)
PO Box 6175
North Plymouth, MA 02362-6175
(608)222-7670 FAX
http://www.autcom.org/
Provides information, support, advocacy, and publications on autism.

Autism Network for Hearing or Visually Impaired Persons
7510 Oceanfront Av
Virginia Beach, VA 23451
(804)428-9036/(804)428-0019 FAX
Dolores and Alan Bartel, Organizers. The network serves as a data bank of families, professionals, and others interested in education, research, and advocacy for those with autism and other sensory disabilities.

Autism Network International
PO Box 35448
Syracuse, NY 13235-5448
http://www.ani.autistics.org
Organization designed for and operated by individuals with autism.

Autism Research Institute
4182 Adams Av
San Diego, California, 92116
(619)281-7165/(619)563-6840 FAX
http://www.autism.com/ari
Bernard Rimland, Director. An information-sharing network for parents and professionals. A priority of the institute is evaluating the various treatments used to help people with autism. Dr. Rimland is one of the leading scientists in the field of biomedical research on autism. Publishes the quarterly newsletter, *Autism Research Review International.*

Autism Services Center/National Autism Hotline
Prichard Bldg
605 9th St
Huntington, WV 25710-0507
(304)525-8014/(304)525-8026 FAX
www.autismservicescenter.org
The Autism Hotline is a free service. The Center provides information, as well as advocacy and consulting services for those involved with autism.

Autism Society of America (ASA)
7910 Woodmont Av, Suite 300
Bethesda, MD 20814
(301)657-0881/(800)3AUTISM
http://www.autism-society.org
A national support group for parents and professionals. Publishes the magazine, *The Advocate*, free with membership. The ASA Information and Referral Service offers information on autism and services for people with autism. Coordinates a network of affiliated local chapters.

Center for the Study of Autism
PO Box 4538
Salem, OR 97302
http://www.autism.org
Stephen M. Edelson, Director. This is an excellent website, providing much information on autism and related links.

Children's Defense Fund
25 East St, NW
Washington, D.C. 20001
(202)628-8787
http://www.childrensdefense.org/contacts.html
A legal organization working to expand the rights of children. Efforts include lobbying and bringing cases to court.

COSAC/The Autism Helpline
1450 Parkside Av, Suite 22
Ewing, NJ 08638
(609)883-8100/(800)4-AUTISM (in NJ)
http://members.aol.com/njautism
COSAC stands for The New Jersey Center for Outreach and Services for the Autism Community and primarily serves the residents of New Jersey. However, out-of-state residents may request information about services for the autistic community through the Autism Helpline and Information Clearinghouse.

Council For Exceptional Children
1920 Association Dr
Reston, VA 20191-1589
(888)CEC-SPED/703-264-9494 FAX
http://www.cec.sped.org/
Committed to improving educational outcomes for individuals with exceptionalities. Provides access to an

international library and database specializing in the education of children with disabilities. Publishers of special education literature *(Journal of Childhood Communication Disorders)*. Write or call for information packet/catalog of products and services.

Cure Autism Now (CAN)
5455 Wilshire Blvd, Suite 715
Los Angeles, CA 90036
(888)8AUTISM/(323)549-0547 FAX
http://www.canfoundation.org
Portia Iversen, Director. An organization founded by parents who are dedicated to finding effective biological treatments and a cure for autism. CAN'S mission is to fund medical research with direct clinical applications in the field of autism. CAN'S Scientific Work Group is made up of top researchers and clinicians, many of whom are parents of children with autism. CAN believes that it is the parents who will mobilize the scientific and medical communities into action.

Developmental Delay Registry
4401 EastWest Hwy, Suite 207
Bethesda, MD 20814
(301)652-2263/(301)652-9133 FAX
http://www.devdelay.org
Patricia Lemer, Director. National registry of children with developmental delays. Conducts research designed to determine if there are ways to prevent developmental delays and help those affected. Offers workshops and seminars. Publishes membership networking directory.

Doug Flutie Jr. Foundation for Autism
PO Box 767
233 Cochituate Rd, 2nd Floor
Framingham, MA 01701

(866)3AUTISM/(508)270-6868 FAX
http://www.dougflutiejrfoundation.org
Provides funding for services for financially disadvantaged families who need assistance in caring for their autistic children, funds research and education, clearinghouse and communications center for new and innovative programs and services.

Family Village
Waisman Center/University of Wisconsin-Madison
1500 Highland Av
Madison, WI 53705-2280
http://www.familyvillage.wisc.edu
Integrates information, resources, and communication opportunities on the Internet. Includes informational resources on specific diagnoses, adaptive products and technology, education, health issues and disability-related media and literature.

Indiana Resource Center for Autism (IRCA)
The Institute for the Study of Developmental Disabilities
2853 E 10th St
Bloomington, IN 47408-2601
(812)855-6508/(812) 855-9630 FAX
http://www.isdd.indiana.edu/~irca/
Offers many excellent materials concerning autism: booklets,videos, teaching modules. Write or call for free information list.

Maap Services, Inc. (MAAP)
PO Box 524
Crown Point, IN 46307
(219)662-1311/(219)662-0638 FAX
http://www.maapservices.org
Publishes quarterly newsletter for parents. Sells information packet, "Tips for Teachers," and a parent handbook.

National Alliance for the Mentally Ill (NAMI)
Colonial Place Three
2107 Wilson Blvd., Suite 300
Arlington, VA 22201
(800)950-NAMI [6264]
http://www.nami.org
A grass-roots, self-help, support, and advocacy organization for families and friends of people of all ages with neurobiological disorders. More than 1,000 affiliates nationwide.

National Association of Developmental Disabilities Councils
1234 Massachusetts Av, NW, Suite 103
Washington, DC 20005
(202)347-1234/(202)347-4023 FAX
http://www.naddc.org
There are DD Councils in each US state and territory. Works with legislatures to advocate for disabled citizens.

National Organization of Protection and Advocacy Systems
900 2nd St, NE, Suite 211
Washington, DC 20002
(202)408-9514
http://www.protectionandadvocacy.com
Provides help with advocacy, special education, and more. Can help locate a state-affiliated agency.

National Information Center for Children and Youth With Disabilities (NICHY)
PO Box 1492
Washington, DC 20013
(800)695-0285/(202)884-8441 FAX
http://www.nichcy.org/
Publishes *NICHY News Digest* (free subscription within

US). Provides free information on autism and other disabilities. Can also help in locating educational programs and services for children with disabilities.

National Organization for Rare Disorders (NORD)
55 Kenosi Avenue
PO Box 1968
Danbury, CT 06813-1968
(800)999-6673/(203)798-2291 FAX
http://www.rarediseases.org
Informational services on many disabilities.

Sibling Support Project
Children's Hospital and Medical Center
PO Box 5371, CL-09
Seattle, WA 98105
(206)527-5712/(206)527-5705 FAX
http://www.chmc.org/departmt/sibsupp
Offers online support information for siblings of people with autism.

Specialized Training of Military Parents (STOMP)
6316 S 12th St
Tacoma, WA 98465-1900
(800)5-PARENT/253-566-8052 FAX
http://www.stompproject.org
Offers support and training for parents (in the military service) of special needs children.

Vaccine Information Center
421-E Church St
Vienna, VA 22180
(703)938-0342/(800)909-SHOT
http://www.909shot.com
Provides information on vaccines as well as referrals to physicians and attorneys. Publishes a newsletter, *The Vaccine Reaction*.

Books, Publications, Products

Autism Asperger's Digest
721 W. Abram
Arlington, TX 76013
http://www.futurehorizons-autism.com
Veronica Palmer, Managing Editor. A bi-monthly collection of outstanding articles on autism & Asperger's syndrome. A reliable source of quality information you can use now and for years to come. $49.95 per year.

Autism Resource Network
904 Main St, Suite 100
Hopkins, MN 55343
(952)988-0088/(612)988-0099 FAX
http://www.autismbooks.com
Cherri Saltzman, Director. A nonprofit organization offering books as well as other products related to autism. The network publishes a quarterly newsletter available for $15 per year.

Autism Society of North Carolina Bookstore
505 Oberlin Rd, Suite 230
Raleigh, NC 27605-1345
(919)743-0204
http://www.autismsociety-nc.org
Can provide over 90 different titles on autism and related topics. Purchase orders from school systems and non-profit organizations are accepted.

Different Roads to Learning
12 West 18th St, Suite 3E
New York, NY 10011
(800)853-1057/(800)317-9146 FAX
http://www.difflearn.com/
Julie Azuma, President. A catalogue offering

skillbuilding toys and playthings focusing on the areas of speech, language, and as cognitive and fine motor skills.

Exceptional Parent Magazine
555 Kinderkamack Rd
Oradell, NJ 07649
(201)634-6550/(201)634-6559 FAX
http://www.eparent.com
Magazine and online resource providing information, support, ideas, encouragement and outreach for parents and families of children with disabilities.

Future Horizons, Inc.
721 W. Abram St
Arlington, TX 76013
(800)489-0727/(817)277-2270 FAX
http://www.futurehorizons-autism.com
Wayne Gilpin, President. Publishes and sells many excellent books and materials specifically on autism. Sponsors autism conferences nationwide.

Journal of Autism and Developmental Disorders
Plenum Publishing Corporation
233 Spring St
New York, NY 10013
(212)620-8000
http://www.plenum.com
Journal focusing on current, professional research on autism.

Locutour Media
1130 Grove St, Suite 300
San Luis Obispo, CA 93401
(800)777-3166/(805) 543-6665 FAX
http://www.learningfundamentals.com
Marna Scarry-Larkin, Director. Offers cognitive rehabilitation CD-ROM technology and other computer software for

developing language skills and cognitive retraining. Train Time® was developed specifically for children with autism.

Miller Educational Tools, Inc.
PO Box 4483
Ft. Lauderdale, FL 33338
(954) 566-6175/(954) 566-7588
http://www.millered.com/
Sally Miller, Founder. Offers POCKETS™, an educational tool designed to assist students in developing and practicing the skills involved in organizing information.

Phat Art 4
PO Box 711
Stratham, NH 03885
(603)778-9990/(603)778-9669 FAX
http://www.phatart4.com
Abby Ward Collins and Sibley Collins, Directors. Offers books on autism and other products that support individuals with autism and their families.

Pro-Ed
8700 Shoal Creek Blvd
Austin, TX 78757
(512)451-3246
Publishes quarterly journal, *Focus on Autism and Other Developmental Disabilities*. Also offers an extensive catalogue of educational materials.

Special Kids Company
PO Box 462
Muskego, WI 53150
(800)KIDS-153
http://www.specialkids1.com
John and Lori Sprecher, Owners. Special Kids offers a large variety of "learning videos" for children with special needs.

Special Needs Project
324 State Street, Suite H
Santa Barbara, CA 93101
(800)333-6867/(805)962-5087
http://www.specialneeds.com/store/
Hod Gray, Director. Offers many books on a wide variety
of disability topics including autism.

St. John's Autism List
listserv@maelstrom.stjohns.edu
http://maelstrom.stjohns.edu/archives/autism.html
An active web list for parents of children with autism.
Sponsored by St. John's University. Send email with the
message: subscribe autism Firstname Surname

Stages Learning Materials
PO Box 27
Chico, CA 95927-0027
(888) 501-8880/(888) 735-7791 FAX
http://www.stageslearning.com/
Angela Nelson, Owner. Offers a complete set of flashcards, featuring shapes, colors, and other objects. The
flashcards are designed to teach a variety of fundamental
language skills to children with speech and language delays or developmental disorders. Free color catalogue
available.

International Listings

Action for Autism
PO Box 3678
Defense Colony
New Dehli 110 024
(91)11-469-0132/(91) 11-469-0132
http://www.autism-india.org

Asperger's Syndrome Support Network (Australia/New Zealand)
PO Box 159
VIRGINIA QLD 4014
http://www.asperger.asn.au

Australian Early Intervention Network
c/o CAMHS
Flinders Medical Centre
Bedford Park, South Australia 5042
Australia
(61)8-8357-5484 FAX
http://auseinet.flinders.edu.au/

Autism-Africa
http://autism-alabama.org/africa/
Collection of links to sites in Africa.

Autism-Europe
Avenue E. Van Beccelaere 26B, Bte 21
B-1170 Brussels
Belgium
32-0-2-675-75-05/32-0-2-675-72-70 FAX
http://www.autismeurope.org

Autism France
182 avenue des Jasmins
06250 Mougins
France
04-93-46-00-48/04-93-46-01-14 FAX
http://www.autisme.france.free.fr

Autism Society of British Columbia
3701 East Hastings, Suite 301
Burnaby, BC
Canada V5C 2H6
(604)434-0880/(604)434-0801 FAX
http://www.autismbc.ca

Autism Society of Canada
PO Box 65
Orangeville, ON. L9W 2Z5
Canada
(519)942-8720/(519)942-3566 FAX
http://autismsocietycanada.ca

Autistic Organization of New Zealand, Inc.
PO Box 7305
Sydenham, Christchurch, New Zealand
(03)332 1038
http://www.autismnz.org.nz/

Barcelona Autism Project
Paseo San Gervasio
90, Local 2
08022
Barcelona, Spain
011-3493-418-4850/011-3493-418-4850 FAX

Center for Autism and Related Disorders (CARD) Australia
Royal Randwick Shopping Center
73 Belmore Rd, Suite 69A
Randwick, NSW 2031 Australia
011-612-931-00022/011-612-931-00233 FAX

Center for Children with Autism (Comunidad Los Horcones)
Carretera a Yecora Km. 63 Hwy 16
Apartado Postal # 372
Hermosillo
Sonora 830000 Mexico
(52) (662) 214-72-19
http://www.loshorcones.org.mx/autismo.html

The Geneva Center
250 Davisville Av, Suite 200
Toronto, Ontario
Canada M4S 1H2
(416)322-7877/(416)322-5894 FAX
http://www.autism.net

Iceland Young Autism Project
Digranesvegur 5
200 Kopavogur
Iceland
011-354-554-5462/011-354-564-1753 FAX

Irish Society for Autism
Unity Building
16/17 Lower O'Connell St
Dublin 1
Republic of Ireland
(071)744684/(071)744244 FAX
http://www.iol.ie/~isa1/

The National Autistic Society UK (NAS)
393 City Rd
London, ECIV ING
United Kingdon
44-0-20-7833-2299/44-0-20-7833-9666
http://www.nas.org.uk

The National Autistic Society in Wales (NASW)
William Knox House
Britannic Way
West Glamorgan, SA10 6EL
Llandarcy, Wales
(01)792 815915

The Scottish Society for Autistic Children
SSAC Headquarters

Hilton House, Alloa Business Park, Whins Rd
Alloa, FK10 3SA Scotland
(01259)720044/(01259)720051 FAX
http://www.autism-in-scotland.org.uk/

Index

A

Allergy-Induced Autism   76
American Academy of Environmental Medicine   77, 86
American Association of Naturopathic Physicians   77, 86
American EPD Society   74, 77
American Music Therapy Association   119
American Occupational Therapy Association   91
American Osteopathic Association   104
Analytical Research Labs   77
anti-anxiety   60
anticonvulsants   60
antidepression   60
antifungal medications   85
Antimania   60
antipsychotics   60
Applied Behavioral Analysis   34–36
Asperger's Syndrome   7, 10, 14, 15, 17, 18
Asperger's Syndrome Coalition of the United States   14, 133
Association for Comprehensive NeuroTherapy   78
Association of University Centers on Disabilities   12

Attwood, Tony   17, 19
Auditory Integration Training   94, 94–95, 96, 97
AutCom   134
Autism/Asperger's Digest   141
Autism, Intolerance, and Allergy (AIA)   78
Autism National Committee   134
Autism Network for Dietary Intervention   78
Autism Network International   134
Autism Research Centre   12
Autism Research Foundation   12
Autism Research Institute   13, 39, 55, 63, 66, 70, 72,
    79, 80, 85, 86–87, 88, 96
Autism Research Review International   49, 55, 57, 58
Autism Research Unit, School of Health Sciences   79
Autism Resource Network   141
Autism Services Center   135
Autism Society of America   13, 40
Autistic Disorder   8
Ayers, Jean   89

B

B6/Magnesium Supplements   50–51
Berard, Guy   94
beta blockers   61
biofeedback   124, 127, 129
Biofeedback Certification Institute of America   127
Biological Treatments for Autism and PDD   86, 88
Biology of the Autistic Syndrome, The (Gillberg)   21
Biomedical Assessment Options for Children with
    Autism   22–23
Biomedical Interventions   59–70
Boston Higashi School   111, 112
Burger School for the Autistic   40

C

candida   83–88
Candida Albicans   83, 85, 87, 88
CANDLE   15
Celiac Disease Foundation   79
Center for Health and Healing   67
Center for Neurodevelopmental Studies   92
Center for Visual Management   100
Checklist for Autism in Toddlers   6
Child with Special Needs   108, 109
Childhood Autism Rating Scale   7, 18
cod liver oil   52–53
Cognitive Concepts Inc.   40
Craniosacral Therapy Association, United Kingdom   104
Cure Autism Now   13, 137

D

Daily Life Therapy   111, 112
Defeat Autism Now (DAN!) Protocol   22–23
Delacato, Carl   113–114
Delacato International   114
Developmental Concepts   92
Developmental Delay Registry   101, 137
Diagnosis   3–19
Diagnostic and Statistical Manual of Mental ...   5, 8
Dietary Interventions   71–82
Different Roads to Learning   141–142
Dimethylglycine   54, 58
Discrete Trial Training   36
Doman, Glenn   113, 114
Doman, Robert   113
Doman/Delacato Method   113–114
Doug Flutie Jr. Foundation for Autism   137–138

E

Early Intervention/Teaching Strategies   31–37
Earobics   38–39, 40
Edelson   94, 95, 96, 97, 101, 102
Education   27–47
Education for All Handicapped Act   28
EEG Spectrum, Inc.   127
ELISA   75, 78
Emergence: Labeled Autistic   125, 128
Epilepsy Foundation   15
Exceptional Parent Magazine   142

F

Families for Early Autism Treatment (FEAT)   26, 35, 41
Family Village   138
FastForword   38
fatty acids   53
Federal Law in the United States   27–31
Feingold Association of the United States   78
First Signs   15
floor-time   108
folic acid   51–52, 54
Form E-2   6
Fragile-X Syndrome   5, 10
Friends of Landau Kleffner Syndrome   16
Future Horizons   19, 46, 68, 81, 141, 142

G

Grandin, Temple   125–127, 129
Gray, Carol   37
Great Plains Laboratory   24, 79, 86, 87
Great Smokies Diagnostic Laboratory   24, 87
Greenspan Method   107–108
Greenspan, Stanley   107, 108

Groden Center 124, 125, 128
Groden, June 124, 128, 129
Gupta, Sudhir 67

H

Handle Institute 41
Honormead Schools Ltd. 112
hug machine 125, 126, 127, 128, 129, 130

I

Immuno Laboratories 24, 80, 87
Immunoglobulin G 64
Indiana Resource Center for Autism 41, 138
Individual Family Services Plan 31
Individualized Education Program (IEP) 29
Individuals With Disabilities Education Act 28
Infantile Autism: The Syndrome and Its Implication 3–4, 18
Institute for the Achievement of Human Potential 113, 114
Intensive Interventions 107–108
International Rett Syndrome Association 16
Irlen Institute 101
Irlen Lenses 99–100
IVIG Therapy 62, 64, 67, 69

J

Journal of Autism and Developmental Disorders 142
Judevine Center for Autism 42

K

Kanner, Leo 3, 7
Kaplan, Melvin 100, 101
KareMor® International 56
Kaufman, Barry Neil 109, 110
Kaufman, Samahria 109

Kirkman Laboratory   50, 55
Kirkman Sales Co.   56, 80
Kitahara, Kiyo   111

L

Landau-Kleffner Syndrome   10, 15
'Leaky Gut' Problem   72–73
Lejeune, Jerome   52
Let Me Hear Your Voice   34, 45
Locutour Media   142
Lovaas Institute for Early Intervention   42
Lovaas, Ivar O.   34

M

M.I.N.D. Institute   14
Medications   60–62
Megson, Mary   52, 56
melatonin   55, 57
Moebius Syndrome   11
Musashino Higashi Gakuen School   112
Music Interventions   117–121
Music Therapy   117–118

N

National Alliance for Autism Research   14
National Alliance for the Mentally Ill   67, 139
National Association of Developmental Disabilities   139
National Autism Hotline   135
National Autistic Society (NAS) UK   14
National Fragile-X Foundation   16
National Information Center for Children and Youth   139
National Organization for Rare Disorders   140

National Organization of Protection and ... 139
New Jersey Center for Outreach and Services ... 32
Nordoff-Robbins Music Therapy Centre 119
North American Riding for the Handicapped ... 92
Nutritional Supplements 49–58
Nystatin 85

O

Opiate Blockers 61
Option Institute and Fellowship 109, 110, 111
Osteopathic Centre for Children 105
osteopathy 103, 104
Osteopathy/Craniosacral SM Therapy 103–104

P

Parents Active for Vision Education 101
PDDNOS 6
Pervasive Developmental Disorder Not Otherwise ... 5, 9
Phat Art 4 143
Picture Exchange Communication System (PECS) 36–37
Pivotal Response Training 36
Progressive Relaxation 124
Project PACE 42
Public Law 101-476 28
Public Law 94-142 28
pyridoxine 49

R

RAST 75
REI Institute 119, 120
related services 28, 29
Relaxation Techniques 123–130
Research and Training Center on Positive Behavioral ... 43
restrictive environment 28

Rett Syndrome 7, 11, 16
Rhythmic Entrainment Intervention 118–119
Rimland, Bernard 49, 55

S

SAMe 54, 55
Scientific Learning Corporation 43
secretin 62–64, 68, 69
sedatives 61
Sensory Integration 89–91
Sensory Integration International 90, 92
Sensory Integration Quarterly 93
Sensory Integrative Therapy 91, 92, 93
Sensory/Physical Therapies 89–91
Sensory Resources 93
Sibling Support Project 140
Social Stories 37–38
Son-Rise Program, The 109–110
Son-Rise: The Miracle Continues 109, 110
Sotos Syndrome 11
Sound of a Miracle: A Child's Triumph over Autism 94, 97
Special Kids Company 143
Special Needs Project 144
Specialized Training of Military Parents 140
squeeze machine 125, 127
St. John's Autism List 144
Stages Learning Materials 144
stimulants 61
Strong, Jeff 118, 120
Structured Teaching 37
Super Nu-Thera® 50

T

TEACCH 37, 43
The ARC 133
The Eden Family of Services 40–41
The Handle Institute 41
The Upledger Institute 105
Therafin Corporation 128
Thinking in Pictures 125, 128
Tourette Syndrome 7, 11, 16
Tourette Syndrome Association 16
Tuberous Sclerosis Alliance 16–17
Transfer Factor 65–66
Trimethylglycine 54

U

University of Kansas 44
Unraveling the Mystery of Autism and Pervasive ... 72, 81
Upledger, John E. 102

V

Vision Therapy and Prism Lenses 97–99
Visual Interventions 97–100
vitamin A 52–53, 56
vitamin B6 49, 50, 56, 57, 58
vitamin C 51, 52, 53, 58

W

Wholesale Nutrition 56
Williams Syndrome 11
Wrightslaw 44

Z

zinc 53, 54

Order Form
Help get the information out!

Order the Autism Treatment Guide for:

- ■ A friend
- ■ A doctor
- ■ A teacher
- ■ A library

- -

Please send me _____ copies at $14.95 each, plus $5.00 per book shipping and handling in U.S. ($10.00 outside U.S.)

Please print clearly

Name _____

Address _____

City/State/Zip _____

Send check and order form to:

FUTURE HORIZONS ᵢₙc

Future Horizons, Inc.
721 W Abram St
Arlington, TX 76013